UK Air Fryer Cookbook for Beginners

Perfectly Easy and Amazing Recipes You Will Love for a Faster and Healthier Lifestyle | Incl. Breakfast, Lunch, Dinner, Snacks and More

Jerry Wong

All Rights Reserved.

The contents of this book may not be reproduced, copied or transmitted without the direct written permission of the author or publisher. Under no circumstances will the publisher or the author be held responsible or liable for any damage, compensation or pecuniary loss arising directly or indirectly from the information contained in this book.

Legal notice. This book is protected by copyright. It is intended for personal use only. You may not modify, distribute, sell, use, quote or paraphrase any part or content of this book without the consent of the author or publisher.

Notice Of Disclaimer.

Please note that the information in this document is intended for educational and entertainment purposes only. Every effort has been made to provide accurate, up-to-date, reliable and complete information. No warranty of any kind is declared or implied. The reader acknowledges that the author does not engage in the provision of legal, financial, medical or professional advice. The content in this book has been obtained from a variety of sources. Please consult a licensed professional before attempting any of the techniques described in this book. By reading this document, the reader agrees that in no event shall the author be liable for any direct or indirect damages, including but not limited to errors, omissions or inaccuracies, resulting from the use of the information in this document.

CONTENTS

INTRODUCTION 10

BREAD AND BREAKFAST 11

Thyme Beef & Eggs 11

Lemon-blueberry Morning Bread 11

Wake-up Veggie & Ham Bake 12

Pizza Dough 12

Garlic Bread Knots 13

Apple French Toast Sandwich 13

Western Frittata 14

Easy Caprese Flatbread 14

Nutty Whole Wheat Muffins 15

Baked Eggs With Bacon-tomato Sauce 15

Cinnamon Pear Oat Muffins 16

Banana-strawberry Cakecups 16

Bacon, Broccoli And Swiss Cheese Bread Pudding 17

Cheddar & Egg Scramble 17

Green Onion Pancakes 18

Eggless Mung Bean Tart 18

Blueberry French Toast Sticks 19

Breakfast Burrito With Sausage 19

Bread Boat Eggs 20

Breakfast Chimichangas 20

APPETIZERS AND SNACKS 21

Caponata Salsa 21

Spicy Chicken And Pepper Jack Cheese Bites 21

Five Spice Fries 22

Honey-lemon Chicken Wings 22

Vegetarian Fritters With Green Dip 23

Vegetable Spring Rolls 23

Poppy Seed Mini Hot Dog Rolls 24

Crab Cake Bites 24

Warm And Salty Edamame 25

Sausage & Cauliflower Balls 25

Middle Eastern Phyllo Rolls 26

Sweet Chili Peanuts 27

Middle Eastern Roasted Chickpeas 27

Grilled Ham & Muenster Cheese On Raisin Bread 27

Kale Chips 28

Chinese-style Potstickers 28

Cheese Straws 29

Cheese Wafers 29

Polenta Fries With Chili-lime Mayo 30

Garlic Breadsticks 30

POULTRY RECIPES 31

Fiery Chicken Meatballs 31

Intense Buffalo Chicken Wings 32

Philly Chicken Cheesesteak Stromboli 32

Farmer's Fried Chicken 33

Crispy "fried" Chicken 33

Buttered Chicken Thighs 34

Yummy Maple-mustard Chicken Kabobs 34

Sunday Chicken Skewers 35

Teriyaki Chicken Bites 35

Country Chicken Hoagies 36

Maple Bacon Wrapped Chicken Breasts 36

Glazed Chicken Thighs 37

Chicken Meatballs With A Surprise 37

Spicy Black Bean Turkey Burgers With Cumin-avocado Spread 37

Poblano Bake 38

Punjabi-inspired Chicken 39

Buttered Turkey Breasts 39

Harissa Chicken Wings 40

Cajun Chicken Livers 40

Basic Chicken Breasts(1) 41

BEEF, PORK & LAMB RECIPES 41

Sweet Potato–crusted Pork Rib Chops 41

Meat Loaves 42

Skirt Steak Fajitas 42

Sirloin Steak Flatbread 43

Chinese-style Lamb Chops 44

Beef Al Carbon (street Taco Meat) 44

Indonesian Pork Satay 44

Balsamic Marinated Rib Eye Steak With Balsamic Fried Cipollini Onions 45

Stress-free Beef Patties 46

Steakhouse Burgers With Red Onion Compote 46

Red Curry Flank Steak 47

Tamari-seasoned Pork Strips 47

Easy Carnitas 48

Skirt Steak With Horseradish Cream 48

Kielbasa Chunks With Pineapple & Peppers 49

Kochukaru Pork Lettuce Cups 49

Lamb Burger With Feta And Olives 50

Crispy Ham And Eggs 51

Peachy Pork Chops 51

Steak Fajitas 52

FISH AND SEAFOOD RECIPES 52

Corn & Shrimp Boil 52

Salmon Puttanesca En Papillotte With Zucchini 53

Cheesy Salmon-stuffed Avocados 53

Breaded Parmesan Perch 54

Shrimp-jalapeño Poppers In Prosciutto 54

Mom´s Tuna Melt Toastie 55

Fried Scallops 55

Sinaloa Fish Fajitas 56

Dilly Red Snapper 56

Piña Colada Shrimp 57

Lime Halibut Parcels 57

Fish Tacos With Hot Coleslaw 58

Seared Scallops In Beurre Blanc 59

Easy Asian-style Tuna 59

Hot Calamari Rings 59

Horseradish Tuna Croquettes 60

Tilapia Al Pesto 60

Holiday Shrimp Scampi 61

Fish And "chips" 61

Lemon-dill Salmon Burgers 62

VEGETARIANS RECIPES 62

Party Giant Nachos 62

Vietnamese Gingered Tofu 63

Falafels 63

Sushi-style Deviled Eggs 64

Vegetarian Shepherd's Pie 64

Spinach & Brie Frittata 65

Cheese Ravioli 65

Crunchy Rice Paper Samosas 66

Roasted Veggie Bowls 67

Veggie Samosas 67

Cheesy Veggie Frittata 67

General Tso's Cauliflower 68

Harissa Veggie Fries 69

Pineapple & Veggie Souvlaki 69

Arancini With Marinara 70

Tropical Salsa 70

Corn And Pepper Jack Chile Rellenos With Roasted Tomato Sauce 71

Cheesy Eggplant Lasagna... 72

Egg Rolls 72

Rigatoni With Roasted Onions, Fennel, Spinach And Lemon Pepper Ricotta 73

VEGETABLE SIDE DISHES RECIPES 74

Garlicky Bell Pepper Mix 74

Thyme Sweet Potato Wedges 74

Teriyaki Tofu With Spicy Mayo 75

Spiced Pumpkin Wedges 75

Sesame Carrots And Sugar Snap Peas 76

Asparagus 76

Balsamic Green Beans With Bacon 77

Buttery Radish Wedges 77

Fried Eggplant Balls 77

Patatas Bravas 78

Rich Baked Sweet Potatoes 78

Green Dip With Pine Nuts 79

Mushrooms, Sautéed ... 79

Easy Parmesan Asparagus ... 79

Rosemary Roasted Potatoes With Lemon ... 80

Lovely Mac`n´cheese ... 80

Citrusy Brussels Sprouts ... 81

Roasted Fennel Salad ... 81

Healthy Caprese Salad ... 82

Buttered Brussels Sprouts ... 82

SANDWICHES AND BURGERS RECIPES ... 82

Thanksgiving Turkey Sandwiches ... 82

Perfect Burgers ... 83

Salmon Burgers ... 84

White Bean Veggie Burgers ... 84

Inside Out Cheeseburgers ... 85

Lamb Burgers ... 85

Sausage And Pepper Heros ... 86

Chicken Spiedies ... 87

Black Bean Veggie Burgers ... 87

Chicken Gyros ... 88

Reuben Sandwiches ... 89

Inside-out Cheeseburgers ... 89

Chicken Saltimbocca Sandwiches ... 90

Best-ever Roast Beef Sandwiches ... 90

Eggplant Parmesan Subs ... 91

Chicken Apple Brie Melt ... 91

Thai-style Pork Sliders ... 92

Mexican Cheeseburgers ... 92

Dijon Thyme Burgers ... 93

Chicken Club Sandwiches ... 94

DESSERTS AND SWEETS 95

Vanilla Butter Cake 95

Peanut Butter S'mores 95

Peanut Butter-banana Roll-ups 96

Coconut-carrot Cupcakes 96

Cinnamon Canned Biscuit Donuts 97

Fall Pumpkin Cake 97

Orange Gooey Butter Cake 98

Giant Oatmeal–peanut Butter Cookie 99

Cheese & Honey Stuffed Figs 99

Party S'mores 100

Baked Apple 100

Easy Bread Pudding 101

Coconut-custard Pie 101

Air-fried Strawberry Hand Tarts 102

Caramel Apple Crumble 102

Fried Pineapple Chunks 103

Oreo-coated Peanut Butter Cups 104

Carrot-oat Cake Muffins 104

Blueberry Cheesecake Tartlets 105

Donut Holes 106

INDEX 107

INTRODUCTION

Did you just get your Air Fryer and wonder where to begin?
Look no further! This cookbook is the perfect guide for taking your air fryer cooking to the next level, with recipes specifically crafted for UK kitchens.

What sets this cookbook apart?

Beginner-Friendly with UK Measurements
Say goodbye to confusing conversions! This cookbook is specifically designed for the UK, with all measurements in familiar units. It's the perfect companion for beginners, ensuring that every recipe is as easy to follow as it is delicious.

Quick, Tasty Meals in 30 Minutes or Less
No time to cook? No problem! Most recipes in this book can be prepared in less than 30 minutes, making it ideal for busy households. You'll be able to create tasty, home-cooked meals without the long prep time.

Delicious & Various Recipes
It offers a wide variety of recipe types, including but not limited to pizza, beef, shrimp, veggies, poultry, and more. Whether you're a breakfast, an afternoon nap, or a late-night snack reveler, you'll find that dish here.

Unusual & Affordable Ingredients
We know that you are budget-conscious, so we have chosen ingredients that are commonly known to our customers so that you don't have to worry about them! We are committed to ensuring every customer enjoys their meal while maximizing costs.

Inside, you'll find:
Enhance your cooking experience and boost your health!
Rich and varied breakfast and dinner recipes
Delicious poultry, pork and beef recipes
Healthy vegetables and side dishes
Delicious seafood for the whole family
Crispy and delicious appetizers and snacks
Healthy baked goods and desserts
And much more!..

Don't miss out on the chance to unlock your air fryer's full potential and cook like a pro!

Click "BUY NOW" before this opportunity slips away!

Bread And Breakfast

Thyme Beef & Eggs

Servings: 1

Cooking Time: 25 Minutes

Ingredients:

- 2 tbsp butter
- 1 rosemary sprig
- 2 garlic cloves, pressed
- 8 oz sirloin steak
- Salt and pepper to taste
- ⅛ tsp cayenne pepper
- 2 eggs
- 1 tsp dried thyme

Directions:

1. Preheat air fryer to 400°F. On a clean cutting board, place butter and half of the rosemary spring in the center. Set aside. Season both sides of the steak with salt, black pepper, thyme, pressed garlic, and cayenne pepper. Transfer the steak to the frying basket and top with the other half of the rosemary sprig. Cook for 4 minutes, then flip the steak. Cook for another 3 minutes.
2. Remove the steak and set it on top of the butter and rosemary sprig on the cutter board. Tent with foil and let it rest. Grease ramekin and crack both eggs into it. Season with salt and pepper. Transfer the ramekin to the frying basket and bake for 4-5 minutes until the egg white is cooked and set. Remove the foil from the steak and slice. Serve with eggs and enjoy.

Lemon-blueberry Morning Bread

Servings: 2

Cooking Time: 15 Minutes

Ingredients:

- ½ cup flour
- ¼ cup powdered sugar
- ½ tsp baking powder
- ⅛ tsp salt
- 2 tbsp butter, melted
- 1 egg
- ½ tsp gelatin
- ½ tsp vanilla extract
- 1 tsp lemon zest
- ½ cup blueberries

Directions:

1. Preheat air fryer to 300°F. Mix the flour, sugar, baking powder, and salt in a bowl. In another bowl, whisk the butter, egg, gelatin, lemon zest, vanilla extract, and blueberries. Add egg mixture to flour mixture and stir until smooth. Spoon mixture into a pizza pan. Place pan in the frying basket and Bake for 10 minutes. Let sit for 5 minutes before slicing. Serve immediately.

Wake-up Veggie & Ham Bake

Servings: 4

Cooking Time: 25 Minutes

Ingredients:

- 25 Brussels sprouts, halved
- 2 mini sweet peppers, diced
- 1 yellow onion, diced
- 3 deli ham slices, diced
- 2 tbsp orange juice
- ¼ tsp salt
- 1 tsp orange zest

Directions:

1. Preheat air fryer to 350ºF. Mix the sprouts, sweet peppers, onion, deli ham, orange juice, and salt in a bowl. Transfer to the frying basket and Air Fry for 12 minutes, tossing once. Scatter with orange zest and serve.

Pizza Dough

Servings: 3

Cooking Time: 10 Minutes

Ingredients:

- 4 cups bread flour, pizza ("00") flour or all-purpose flour
- 1 teaspoon active dry yeast
- 2 teaspoons sugar
- 2 teaspoons salt
- 1½ cups water
- 1 tablespoon olive oil

Directions:

1. Combine the flour, yeast, sugar and salt in the bowl of a stand mixer. Add the olive oil to the flour mixture and start to mix using the dough hook attachment. As you're mixing, add 1¼ cups of the water, mixing until the dough comes together. Continue to knead the dough with the dough hook for another 10 minutes, adding enough water to the dough to get it to the right consistency.
2. Transfer the dough to a floured counter and divide it into 3 equal portions. Roll each portion into a ball. Lightly coat each dough ball with oil and transfer to the refrigerator, covered with plastic wrap. You can place them all on a baking sheet, or place each dough ball into its own oiled zipper sealable plastic bag or container. (You can freeze the dough balls at this stage, removing as much air as possible from the oiled bag.) Keep in the refrigerator for at least one day, or as long as five days.
3. When you're ready to use the dough, remove your dough from the refrigerator at least 1 hour prior to baking and let it sit on the counter, covered gently with plastic wrap.

Garlic Bread Knots

Servings: 8

Cooking Time: 5 Minutes

Ingredients:

- ¼ cup melted butter
- 2 teaspoons garlic powder
- 1 teaspoon dried parsley
- 1 (11-ounce) tube of refrigerated French bread dough

Directions:

1. Mix the melted butter, garlic powder and dried parsley in a small bowl and set it aside.
2. To make smaller knots, cut the long tube of bread dough into 16 slices. If you want to make bigger knots, slice the dough into 8 slices. Shape each slice into a long rope about 6 inches long by rolling it on a flat surface with the palm of your hands. Tie each rope into a knot and place them on a plate.
3. Preheat the air fryer to 350°F.
4. Transfer half of the bread knots into the air fryer basket, leaving space in between each knot. Brush each knot with the butter mixture using a pastry brush.
5. Air-fry for 5 minutes. Remove the baked knots and brush a little more of the garlic butter mixture on each. Repeat with the remaining bread knots and serve warm.

Apple French Toast Sandwich

Servings: 1

Cooking Time: 30 Minutes

Ingredients:

- 2 white bread slices
- 2 eggs
- 1 tsp cinnamon
- ½ peeled apple, sliced
- 1 tbsp brown sugar
- ¼ cup whipped cream

Directions:

1. Preheat air fryer to 350°F. Coat the apple slices with brown sugar in a small bowl. Whisk the eggs and cinnamon into a separate bowl until fluffy and completely blended. Coat the bread slices with the egg mixture, then place them on the greased frying basket. Top with apple slices and Air Fry for 20 minutes, flipping once until the bread is brown nicely and the apple is crispy.
2. Place one French toast slice onto a serving plate, then spoon the whipped cream on top and spread evenly. Scoop the caramelized apple slices onto the whipped cream, and cover with the second toast slice. Serve.

Western Frittata

Servings: 1

Cooking Time: 19 Minutes

Ingredients:

- ½ red or green bell pepper, cut into ½-inch chunks
- 1 teaspoon olive oil
- 3 eggs, beaten
- ¼ cup grated Cheddar cheese
- ¼ cup diced cooked ham
- salt and freshly ground black pepper, to taste
- 1 teaspoon butter
- 1 teaspoon chopped fresh parsley

Directions:

1. Preheat the air fryer to 400°F.
2. Toss the peppers with the olive oil and air-fry for 6 minutes, shaking the basket once or twice during the cooking process to redistribute the ingredients.
3. While the vegetables are cooking, beat the eggs well in a bowl, stir in the Cheddar cheese and ham, and season with salt and freshly ground black pepper. Add the air-fried peppers to this bowl when they have finished cooking.
4. Place a 6- or 7-inch non-stick metal cake pan into the air fryer basket with the butter using an aluminum sling to lower the pan into the basket. (Fold a piece of aluminum foil into a strip about 2-inches wide by 24-inches long.) Air-fry for 1 minute at 380°F to melt the butter. Remove the cake pan and rotate the pan to distribute the butter and grease the pan. Pour the egg mixture into the cake pan and return the pan to the air fryer, using the aluminum sling.
5. Air-fry at 380°F for 12 minutes, or until the frittata has puffed up and is lightly browned. Let the frittata sit in the air fryer for 5 minutes to cool to an edible temperature and set up. Remove the cake pan from the air fryer, sprinkle with parsley and serve immediately.

Easy Caprese Flatbread

Servings: 2

Cooking Time: 15 Minutes

Ingredients:

- 1 fresh mozzarella ball, sliced
- 1 flatbread
- 2 tsp olive oil
- ¼ garlic clove, minced
- 1 egg
- ⅛ tsp salt
- ¼ cup diced tomato
- 6 basil leaves
- ½ tsp dried oregano
- ½ tsp balsamic vinegar

Directions:

1. Preheat air fryer to 380°F. Lightly brush the top of the bread with olive oil, then top with garlic. Crack the egg into a small bowl and sprinkle with salt. Place the bread into the frying basket and gently pour the egg onto the top of the pita. Top with tomato, mozzarella, oregano and basil. Bake for 6 minutes. When ready, remove the pita pizza and drizzle with balsamic vinegar. Let it cool for 5 minutes. Slice and serve.

Nutty Whole Wheat Muffins

Servings: 8

Cooking Time: 11 Minutes

Ingredients:

- ½ cup whole-wheat flour, plus 2 tablespoons
- ¼ cup oat bran
- 2 tablespoons flaxseed meal
- ¼ cup brown sugar
- ½ teaspoon baking soda
- ½ teaspoon baking powder
- ¼ teaspoon salt
- ½ teaspoon cinnamon
- ½ cup buttermilk
- 2 tablespoons melted butter
- 1 egg
- ½ teaspoon pure vanilla extract
- ½ cup grated carrots
- ¼ cup chopped pecans
- ¼ cup chopped walnuts
- 1 tablespoon pumpkin seeds
- 1 tablespoon sunflower seeds
- 16 foil muffin cups, paper liners removed
- cooking spray

Directions:

1. Preheat air fryer to 330°F.
2. In a large bowl, stir together the flour, bran, flaxseed meal, sugar, baking soda, baking powder, salt, and cinnamon.
3. In a medium bowl, beat together the buttermilk, butter, egg, and vanilla. Pour into flour mixture and stir just until dry ingredients moisten. Do not beat.
4. Gently stir in carrots, nuts, and seeds.
5. Double up the foil cups so you have 8 total and spray with cooking spray.
6. Place 4 foil cups in air fryer basket and divide half the batter among them.
7. Cook at 330°F for 11minutes or until toothpick inserted in center comes out clean.
8. Repeat step 7 to cook remaining 4 muffins.

Baked Eggs With Bacon-tomato Sauce

Servings: 1

Cooking Time: 12 Minutes

Ingredients:

- 1 teaspoon olive oil
- 2 tablespoons finely chopped onion
- 1 teaspoon chopped fresh oregano
- pinch crushed red pepper flakes
- 1 (14-ounce) can crushed or diced tomatoes
- salt and freshly ground black pepper
- 2 slices of bacon, chopped
- 2 large eggs
- ¼ cup grated Cheddar cheese
- fresh parsley, chopped

Directions:

1. Start by making the tomato sauce. Preheat a medium saucepan over medium heat on the stovetop. Add the olive oil and sauté the onion, oregano and pepper flakes for 5 minutes. Add the tomatoes and bring to a simmer. Season with salt and freshly ground black pepper and simmer for 10 minutes.
2. Meanwhile, Preheat the air fryer to 400°F and pour a little water into the bottom of the air fryer drawer. (This will help prevent the grease that drips into the bottom drawer from burning and smoking.) Place the bacon in the air fryer basket and air-fry at 400°F for 5 minutes, shaking the basket every once in a while.
3. When the bacon is almost crispy, remove it to a paper-towel lined plate and rinse out the air fryer drawer, draining away the bacon grease.

4. Transfer the tomato sauce to a shallow 7-inch pie dish. Crack the eggs on top of the sauce and scatter the cooked bacon back on top. Season with salt and freshly ground black pepper and transfer the pie dish into the air fryer basket. You can use an aluminum foil sling to help with this by taking a long piece of aluminum foil, folding it in half lengthwise twice until it is roughly 26-inches by 3-inches. Place this under the pie dish and hold the ends of the foil to move the pie dish in and out of the air fryer basket. Tuck the ends of the foil beside the pie dish while it cooks in the air fryer.
5. Air-fry at 400°F for 5 minutes, or until the eggs are almost cooked to your liking. Sprinkle cheese on top and air-fry for an additional 2 minutes. When the cheese has melted, remove the pie dish from the air fryer, sprinkle with a little chopped parsley and let the eggs cool for a few minutes – just enough time to toast some buttered bread in your air fryer!

Cinnamon Pear Oat Muffins

Servings: 6

Cooking Time: 30 Minutes + Cooling Time

Ingredients:

- ½ cup apple sauce
- 1 large egg
- 1/3 cup brown sugar
- 2 tbsp butter, melted
- ½ cup milk
- 11/3 cups rolled oats
- 1 tsp ground cinnamon
- ½ tsp baking powder
- Pinch of salt
- ½ cup diced peeled pears

Directions:

1. Preheat the air fryer to 350°F. Place the apple sauce, egg, brown sugar, melted butter, and milk into a bowl and mix to combine. Stir in the oats, cinnamon, baking powder, and salt and mix well, then fold in the pears.
2. Grease 6 silicone muffin cups with baking spray, then spoon the batter in equal portions into the cups. Put the muffin cups in the frying basket and Bake for 13-18 minutes or until set. Leave to cool for 15 minutes. Serve.

Banana-strawberry Cakecups

Servings: 6

Cooking Time: 25 Minutes

Ingredients:

- ½ cup mashed bananas
- ¼ cup maple syrup
- ½ cup Greek yogurt
- 1 tsp vanilla extract
- 1 egg
- 1 ½ cups flour
- 1 tbsp cornstarch
- ½ tsp baking soda
- ½ tsp baking powder
- ½ tsp salt
- ½ cup strawberries, sliced

Directions:

1. Preheat air fryer to 360°F. Place the mashed bananas, maple syrup, yogurt, vanilla, and egg in a large bowl and mix until smooth. Sift in 1 ½ cups of the flour, baking soda, baking powder, and salt, then stir to combine.
2. In a small bowl, toss the strawberries with the cornstarch. Fold the mixture into the muffin batter. Divide the mixture evenly between greased muffin cups and place into the air frying basket. Bake for 12-15 minutes until golden brown on top and a toothpick inserted into the middle of one of the muffins comes out clean. Leave to cool for 5 minutes. Serve and enjoy!

Bacon, Broccoli And Swiss Cheese Bread Pudding

Servings: 2

Cooking Time: 48 Minutes

Ingredients:

- ½ pound thick cut bacon, cut into ¼-inch pieces
- 3 cups brioche bread or rolls, cut into ½-inch cubes
- 3 eggs
- 1 cup milk
- ½ teaspoon salt
- freshly ground black pepper
- 1 cup frozen broccoli florets, thawed and chopped
- 1½ cups grated Swiss cheese

Directions:

1. Preheat the air fryer to 400°F.
2. Air-fry the bacon for 6 minutes until crispy, shaking the basket a few times while it cooks to help it cook evenly. Remove the bacon and set it aside on a paper towel.
3. Air-fry the brioche bread cubes for 2 minutes to dry and toast lightly. (If your brioche is a few days old and slightly stale, you can omit this step.)
4. Butter a 6- or 7-inch cake pan. Combine all the ingredients in a large bowl and toss well. Transfer the mixture to the buttered cake pan, cover with aluminum foil and refrigerate the bread pudding overnight, or for at least 8 hours.
5. Remove the casserole from the refrigerator an hour before you plan to cook, and let it sit on the countertop to come to room temperature.
6. Preheat the air fryer to 330°F. Transfer the covered cake pan, to the basket of the air fryer, lowering the dish into the basket using a sling made of aluminum foil (fold a piece of aluminum foil into a strip about 2-inches wide by 24-inches long). Fold the ends of the aluminum foil over the top of the dish before returning the basket to the air fryer. Air-fry for 20 minutes. Remove the foil and air-fry for an additional 20 minutes. If the top starts to brown a little too much before the custard has set, simply return the foil to the pan. The bread pudding has cooked through when a skewer inserted into the center comes out clean.

Cheddar & Egg Scramble

Servings: 4

Cooking Time: 20 Minutes

Ingredients:

- 8 eggs
- ¼ cup buttermilk
- ¼ cup milk
- Salt and pepper to taste
- 3 tbsp butter, melted
- 1 cup grated cheddar
- 1 tbsp minced parsley

Directions:

1. Preheat the air fryer to 350°F. Whisk the eggs with buttermilk, milk, salt, and pepper until foamy and set aside. Put the melted butter in a cake pan and pour in the egg mixture. Return the pan into the fryer and cook for 7 minutes, stirring occasionally. Stir in the cheddar cheese and cook for 2-4 more minutes or until the eggs have set. Remove the cake pan and scoop the eggs into a serving plate. Scatter with freshly minced parsley and serve.

Green Onion Pancakes

Servings: 4

Cooking Time: 8 Minutes

Ingredients:

- 2 cup all-purpose flour
- ½ teaspoon salt
- ¾ cup hot water
- 1 tablespoon vegetable oil
- 1 tablespoon butter, melted
- 2 cups finely chopped green onions
- 1 tablespoon black sesame seeds, for garnish

Directions:

1. In a large bowl, whisk together the flour and salt. Make a well in the center and pour in the hot water. Quickly stir the flour mixture together until a dough forms. Knead the dough for 5 minutes; then cover with a warm, wet towel and set aside for 30 minutes to rest.
2. In a small bowl, mix together the vegetable oil and melted butter.
3. On a floured surface, place the dough and cut it into 8 pieces. Working with 1 piece of dough at a time, use a rolling pin to roll out the dough until it's ¼ inch thick; then brush the surface with the oil and butter mixture and sprinkle with green onions. Next, fold the dough in half and then in half again. Roll out the dough again until it's ¼ inch thick and brush with the oil and butter mixture and green onions. Fold the dough in half and then in half again and roll out one last time until it's ¼ inch thick. Repeat this technique with all 8 pieces.
4. Meanwhile, preheat the air fryer to 400°F.
5. Place 1 or 2 pancakes into the air fryer basket (or as many as will fit in your fryer), and cook for 2 minutes or until crispy and golden brown. Repeat until all the pancakes are cooked. Top with black sesame seeds for garnish, if desired.

Eggless Mung Bean Tart

Servings: 2

Cooking Time: 20 Minutes

Ingredients:

- 2 tsp soy sauce
- 1 tsp lime juice
- 1 large garlic clove, minced or pressed
- ½ tsp red chili flakes
- ½ cup mung beans, soaked
- Salt and pepper to taste
- ½ minced shallot
- 1 green onion, chopped

Directions:

1. Preheat the air fryer to 390°F. Add the soy sauce, lime juice, garlic, and chili flakes to a bowl and stir. Set aside.Place the drained beans in a blender along with ½ cup of water, salt, and pepper. Blend until smooth. Stir in shallot and green onion, but do not blend.
2. Pour the batter into a greased baking pan. Bake for 15 minutes in the air fryer until golden. A knife inserted in the center should come out clean. Once cooked, cut the "quiche" into quarters. Drizzle with sauce and serve.

Blueberry French Toast Sticks

Servings: 4

Cooking Time: 20 Minutes

Ingredients:

- 3 bread slices, cut into strips
- 1 tbsp butter, melted
- 2 eggs
- 1 tbsp milk
- 1 tbsp sugar
- ½ tsp vanilla extract
- 1 cup fresh blueberries
- 1 tbsp lemon juice

Directions:

1. Preheat air fryer to 380°F. After laying the bread strips on a plate, sprinkle some melted butter over each piece. Whisk the eggs, milk, vanilla, and sugar, then dip the bread in the mix. Place on a wire rack to let the batter drip. Put the bread strips in the air fryer and Air Fry for 5-7 minutes. Use tongs to flip them once and cook until golden. With a fork, smash the blueberries and lemon juice together. Spoon the blueberries sauce over the French sticks. Serve immediately.

Breakfast Burrito With Sausage

Servings: 6

Cooking Time: 35 Minutes

Ingredients:

- 2 tbsp olive oil
- Salt and pepper to taste
- 6 eggs, beaten
- ½ chopped red bell pepper
- ½ chopped green bell pepper
- 1 onion, finely chopped
- 8 oz chicken sausage
- ½ cup salsa
- 6 flour tortillas
- ½ cup grated cheddar

Directions:

1. Warm the olive oil in a skillet over medium heat. Add the eggs and stir-fry them for 2-3 minutes until scrambled. Season with salt and pepper and set aside.
2. Sauté the bell peppers and onion in the same skillet for 2-3 minutes until tender. Add and brown the chicken sausage, breaking into small pieces with a wooden spoon, about 4 minutes. Return the scrambled eggs and stir in the salsa. Remove the skillet from heat. Divide the mixture between the tortillas. Fold up the top and bottom edges, then roll to fully enclose the filling. Secure with toothpicks. Spritz with cooking spray.
3. Preheat air fryer to 400°F. Bake the burritos in the air fryer for 10 minutes, turning them once halfway through cooking until crisp. Garnish with cheddar cheese. Serve.

Bread Boat Eggs

Servings: 4

Cooking Time: 10 Minutes

Ingredients:

- 4 pistolette rolls
- 1 teaspoon butter
- ¼ cup diced fresh mushrooms
- ½ teaspoon dried onion flakes
- 4 eggs
- ½ teaspoon salt
- ¼ teaspoon dried dill weed
- ¼ teaspoon dried parsley
- 1 tablespoon milk

Directions:

1. Cut a rectangle in the top of each roll and scoop out center, leaving ½-inch shell on the sides and bottom.
2. Place butter, mushrooms, and dried onion in air fryer baking pan and cook for 1 minute. Stir and cook 3 moreminutes.
3. In a medium bowl, beat together the eggs, salt, dill, parsley, and milk. Pour mixture into pan with mushrooms.
4. Cook at 390°F for 2minutes. Stir. Continue cooking for 3 or 4minutes, stirring every minute, until eggs are scrambled to your liking.
5. Remove baking pan from air fryer and fill rolls with scrambled egg mixture.
6. Place filled rolls in air fryer basket and cook at 390°F for 2 to 3minutes or until rolls are lightly browned.

Breakfast Chimichangas

Servings: 4

Cooking Time: 8 Minutes

Ingredients:

- Four 8-inch flour tortillas
- ½ cup canned refried beans
- 1 cup scrambled eggs
- ½ cup grated cheddar or Monterey jack cheese
- 1 tablespoon vegetable oil
- 1 cup salsa

Directions:

1. Lay the flour tortillas out flat on a cutting board. In the center of each tortilla, spread 2 tablespoons refried beans. Next, add ¼ cup eggs and 2 tablespoons cheese to each tortilla.
2. To fold the tortillas, begin on the left side and fold to the center. Then fold the right side into the center. Next fold the bottom and top down and roll over to completely seal the chimichanga. Using a pastry brush or oil mister, brush the tops of the tortilla packages with oil.
3. Preheat the air fryer to 400°F for 4 minutes. Place the chimichangas into the air fryer basket, seam side down, and air fry for 4 minutes. Using tongs, turn over the chimichangas and cook for an additional 2 to 3 minutes or until light golden brown.

Appetizers And Snacks

Caponata Salsa

Servings: 6

Cooking Time: 16 Minutes

Ingredients:

- 4 cups (one 1-pound eggplant) Purple Italian eggplant(s), stemmed and diced (no need to peel)
- Olive oil spray
- 1½ cups Celery, thinly sliced
- 16 (about ½ pound) Cherry or grape tomatoes, halved
- 1 tablespoon Drained and rinsed capers, chopped
- Up to 1 tablespoon Minced fresh rosemary leaves
- 1½ tablespoons Red wine vinegar
- 1½ teaspoons Granulated white sugar
- ¾ teaspoon Table salt
- ¾ teaspoon Ground black pepper

Directions:

1. Preheat the air fryer to 350°F.
2. Put the eggplant pieces in a bowl and generously coat them with olive oil spray. Toss and stir, spray again, and toss some more, until the pieces are glistening.
3. When the machine is at temperature, pour the eggplant pieces into the basket and spread them out into an even layer. Air-fry for 8 minutes, tossing and rearranging the pieces twice.
4. Meanwhile, put the celery and tomatoes in the same bowl the eggplant pieces had been in. Generously coat them with olive oil spray; then toss well, spray again, and toss some more, until the vegetables are well coated.
5. When the eggplant has cooked for 8 minutes, pour the celery and tomatoes on top in the basket. Air-fry undisturbed for 8 minutes more, until the tomatoes have begun to soften.
6. Pour the contents of the basket back into the same bowl. Add the capers, rosemary, vinegar, sugar, salt, and pepper. Toss well to blend, breaking up the tomatoes a bit to create more moisture in the mixture.
7. Cover and refrigerate for 2 hours to blend the flavors. Serve chilled or at room temperature. The caponata salsa can stay in its covered bowl in the fridge for up to 2 days before the vegetables weep too much moisture and the dish becomes too wet.

Spicy Chicken And Pepper Jack Cheese Bites

Servings: 8

Cooking Time: 8 Minutes

Ingredients:

- 8 ounces cream cheese, softened
- 2 cups grated pepper jack cheese
- 1 Jalapeño pepper, diced
- 2 scallions, minced
- 1 teaspoon paprika

- 2 teaspoons salt, divided
- 3 cups shredded cooked chicken
- ¼ cup all-purpose flour*
- 2 eggs, lightly beaten
- 1 cup panko breadcrumbs*
- olive oil, in a spray bottle
- salsa

Directions:

1. Beat the cream cheese in a bowl until it is smooth and easy to stir. Add the pepper jack cheese, Jalapeño pepper, scallions, paprika and 1 teaspoon of salt. Fold in the shredded cooked chicken and combine well. Roll this mixture into 1-inch balls.
2. Set up a dredging station with three shallow dishes. Place the flour into one shallow dish. Place the eggs into a second shallow dish. Finally, combine the panko breadcrumbs and remaining teaspoon of salt in a third dish.
3. Coat the chicken cheese balls by rolling each ball in the flour first, then dip them into the eggs and finally roll them in the panko breadcrumbs to coat all sides. Refrigerate for at least 30 minutes.
4. Preheat the air fryer to 400°F.
5. Spray the chicken cheese balls with oil and air-fry in batches for 8 minutes. Shake the basket a few times throughout the cooking process to help the balls brown evenly.
6. Serve hot with salsa on the side.

Five Spice Fries

Servings: 2

Cooking Time: 30 Minutes

Ingredients:

- 1 Yukon Gold potato, cut into fries
- 1 tbsp coconut oil
- 1 tsp coconut sugar
- 1 tsp garlic powder
- ½ tsp Chinese five-spice
- Salt to taste
- ¼ tsp turmeric
- ¼ tsp paprika

Directions:

1. Preheat air fryer to 390°F. Toss the potato pieces with coconut oil, sugar, garlic, Chinese five-spice, salt, turmeric, and paprika in a bowl and stir well. Place in the greased frying basket and Air Fry for 18-25 minutes, tossing twice until softened and golden. Serve warm.

Honey-lemon Chicken Wings

Servings: 4

Cooking Time: 30 Minutes

Ingredients:

- 8 chicken wings
- Salt and pepper to taste

- 3 tbsp honey
- 1 tbsp lemon juice
- 1 tbsp chicken stock
- 2 cloves garlic, minced
- 2 thinly sliced green onions
- ¾ cup barbecue sauce
- 1 tbsp sesame seeds

Directions:

1. Preheat air fryer to 390°F. Season the wings with salt and pepper and place them in the frying basket. Air Fry for 20 minutes. Shake the basket a couple of times during cooking. In a bowl, mix the honey, lemon juice, chicken stock, and garlic. Take the wings out of the fryer and place them in a baking pan. Add the sauce and toss, coating completely. Put the pan in the air fryer and Air Fry for 4-5 minutes until golden and cooked through, with no pink showing. Top with green onions and sesame seeds, then serve with BBQ sauce.

Vegetarian Fritters With Green Dip

Servings: 6

Cooking Time: 40 Minutes

Ingredients:

- ½ cup grated carrots
- ½ cup grated zucchini
- ¼ cup minced yellow onion
- 1 garlic clove, minced
- 1 large egg
- ¼ cup flour
- ¼ cup bread crumbs
- Salt and pepper to taste
- ½ tsp ground cumin
- ½ avocado, peeled and pitted
- ½ cup plain Greek yogurt
- 1 tsp lime juice
- 1 tbsp white vinegar
- ¼ cup chopped cilantro

Directions:

1. Preheat air fryer to 375°F. Combine carrots, zucchini, onion, garlic, egg, flour, bread crumbs, salt, pepper, and cumin in a large bowl. Scoop out 12 equal portions of the vegetables and form them into patties. Arrange the patties on the greased basket. Air Fry for 5 minutes, then flip the patties. Air Fry for another 5 minutes. Check if the fritters are golden and cooked through. If more time is needed, cook for another 3-5 minutes.
2. While the fritters are cooking, prepare the avocado sauce. Mash the avocado in a small bowl to the desired texture. Stir in yogurt, white vinegar, chopped cilantro, lime juice, and salt. When the fritter is done, transfer to a serving plate along with the avocado sauce for dipping. Serve warm and enjoy.

Vegetable Spring Rolls

Servings: 6

Cooking Time: 8 Minutes

Ingredients:

- ¾ cup (a little more than 2½ ounces) Fresh bean sprouts
- 6 tablespoons Shredded carrots
- 6 tablespoons Slivered, drained, sliced canned bamboo shoots
- 1½ tablespoons Regular or low-sodium soy sauce or gluten-free tamari sauce
- 1½ teaspoons Granulated white sugar
- 1½ teaspoons Toasted sesame oil
- 6 Spring roll wrappers (gluten-free, if a concern)
- 1 Large egg, well beaten
- Vegetable oil spray

Directions:

1. Gently stir the bean sprouts, carrots, bamboo shoots, soy or tamari sauce, sugar, and oil in a large bowl until the vegetables are evenly coated. Set aside at room temperature for 10 to 15 minutes.
2. Preheat the air fryer to 400°F.
3. Set a spring roll wrapper on a clean, dry work surface. Pick up about ¼ cup of the vegetable mixture and gently squeeze it in your clean hand to release most of the liquid. Set this bundle of vegetables along one edge of the wrapper.
4. Fold two opposing sides (at right angles to the filling) up and over the filling, concealing part of it and making a folded-over border down two sides of the wrapper. Brush the top half of the wrapper (including the folded parts) with beaten egg so it will seal when you roll it closed.
5. Starting with the side nearest the filling, roll the wrapper closed, working to make a tight fit, eliminating as much air as possible from inside the wrapper. Set it aside seam side down and continue making more filled rolls using the same techniques.
6. Lightly coat all the sealed rolls with vegetable oil spray on all sides. Set them seam side down in the basket and air-fry undisturbed for 8 minutes, or until golden brown and very crisp.
7. Use a nonstick-safe spatula and a flatware fork for balance to transfer the rolls to a wire rack. Cool for at least 5 minutes or up to 15 minutes before serving.

Poppy Seed Mini Hot Dog Rolls

Servings: 4

Cooking Time: 25 Minutes

Ingredients:

- 8 small mini hot dogs
- 8 pastry dough sheets
- 1 tbsp vegetable oil
- 1 tbsp poppy seeds

Directions:

1. Preheat the air fryer to 350°F. Roll the mini hot dogs into a pastry dough sheet, wrapping them snugly. Brush the rolls with vegetable oil on all sides. Arrange them on the frying basket and sprinkle poppy seeds on top. Bake for 15 minutes until the pastry crust is golden brown. Serve.

Crab Cake Bites

Servings: 6

Cooking Time: 20 Minutes

Ingredients:

- 8 oz lump crab meat
- 1 diced red bell pepper
- 1 spring onion, diced
- 1 garlic clove, minced
- 1 tbsp capers, minced
- 1 tbsp cream cheese
- 1 egg, beaten
- ¼ cup bread crumbs
- ¼ tsp salt
- 1 tbsp olive oil
- 1 lemon, cut into wedges

Directions:
1. Preheat air fryer to 360°F. Combine the crab, bell pepper, spring onion, garlic, and capers in a bowl until combined. Stir in the cream cheese and egg. Mix in the bread crumbs and salt. Divide this mixture into 6 equal portions and pat out into patties. Put the crab cakes into the frying basket in a single layer. Drizzle the tops of each patty with a bit of olive oil and Bake for 10 minutes. Serve with lemon wedges on the side. Enjoy!

Warm And Salty Edamame

Servings: 4

Cooking Time: 10 Minutes

Ingredients:

- 1 pound Unshelled edamame
- Vegetable oil spray
- ¾ teaspoon Coarse sea salt or kosher salt

Directions:
1. Preheat the air fryer to 400°F.
2. Place the edamame in a large bowl and lightly coat them with vegetable oil spray. Toss well, spray again, and toss until they are evenly coated.
3. When the machine is at temperature, pour the edamame into the basket and air-fry, tossing the basket quite often to rearrange the edamame, for 7 minutes, or until warm and aromatic. (Air-fry for 10 minutes if the edamame were frozen and not thawed.)
4. Pour the edamame into a bowl and sprinkle the salt on top. Toss well, then set aside for a couple of minutes before serving with an empty bowl on the side for the pods.

Sausage & Cauliflower Balls

Servings: 4

Cooking Time: 30 Minutes

Ingredients:

- 2 chicken sausage links, casings removed
- 1 cup shredded Monterey jack cheese
- 4 ½ cups riced cauliflower
- ½ tsp salt
- 1 ¼ cups pizza sauce
- 2 eggs

- ½ cup breadcrumbs
- 3 tsp grated Parmesan cheese

Directions:

1. In a large skillet over high heat, cook the sausages while breaking them up into smaller pieces with a spoon. Cook through completely for 4 minutes. Add cauliflower, salt, and ¼ cup of pizza sauce. Lower heat to medium and stir-fry for 7 minutes or until the cauliflower is tender. Remove from heat and stir in Monterey cheese. Allow to cool slightly, 4 minutes or until it is easy to handle.
2. Lightly coat a ¼-cup measuring cup with cooking spray. Pack and level the cup with the cauliflower mixture. Remove from the cup and roll it into a ball in your palm. Set aside and repeat until you have 12 balls. In a bowl, beat eggs and 1 tbsp of water until combined. In another bowl, combine breadcrumbs and Parmesan. Dip one cauliflower ball into the egg mixture, then in the crumbs. Press the crumbs so that they stick to the ball. Put onto a workspace and spray with cooking oil. Repeat for all balls.
3. Preheat air fryer to 400°F. Place the balls on the bottom of the frying basket in a single layer. Air Fry for about 8-10 minutes, flipping once until the crumbs are golden and the balls are hot throughout. Warm up the remaining pizza sauce as a dip.

Middle Eastern Phyllo Rolls

Servings: 6

Cooking Time: 5 Minutes

Ingredients:

- 6 ounces Lean ground beef or ground lamb
- 3 tablespoons Sliced almonds
- 1 tablespoon Chutney (any variety), finely chopped
- ¼ teaspoon Ground cinnamon
- ¼ teaspoon Ground coriander
- ¼ teaspoon Ground cumin
- ¼ teaspoon Ground dried turmeric
- ¼ teaspoon Table salt
- ¼ teaspoon Ground black pepper
- 6 18 × 14-inch phyllo sheets (thawed, if necessary)
- Olive oil spray

Directions:

1. Set a medium skillet over medium heat for a minute or two, then crumble in the ground meat. Cook for 3 minutes, stirring often, or until well browned. Stir in the almonds, chutney, cinnamon, coriander, cumin, turmeric, salt, and pepper until well combined. Remove from the heat, scrape the cooked ground meat mixture into a bowl, and cool for 15 minutes.
2. Preheat the air fryer to 400°F.
3. Place one sheet of phyllo dough on a clean, dry work surface. (Keep the others covered.) Lightly coat it with olive oil spray, then fold it in half by bringing the short ends together. Place about 3 tablespoons of the ground meat mixture along one of the longer edges, then fold both of the shorter sides of the dough up and over the meat to partially enclose it (and become a border along the sheet of dough). Roll the dough closed, coat it with olive oil spray on all sides, and set it aside seam side down. Repeat this filling and spraying process with the remaining phyllo sheets.
4. Set the rolls seam side down in the basket in one layer with some air space between them. Air-fry undisturbed for 5 minutes, or until very crisp and golden brown.
5. Use kitchen tongs to transfer the rolls to a wire rack. Cool for only 2 or 3 minutes before serving hot.

Sweet Chili Peanuts

Servings: 6

Cooking Time: 5 Minutes

Ingredients:

- 2 cups (10 ounces) Shelled raw peanuts
- 2 tablespoons Granulated white sugar
- 2 teaspoons Hot red pepper sauce, such as Cholula or Tabasco (gluten-free, if a concern)

Directions:

1. Preheat the air fryer to 400°F.
2. Toss the peanuts, sugar, and hot pepper sauce in a bowl until the peanuts are well coated.
3. When the machine is at temperature, pour the peanuts into the basket, spreading them into one layer as much as you can. Air-fry undisturbed for 3 minutes.
4. Shake the basket to rearrange the peanuts. Continue air-frying for 2 minutes more, shaking and stirring the peanuts every 30 seconds, until golden brown.
5. Pour the peanuts onto a large lipped baking sheet. Spread them into one layer and cool for 5 minutes before serving.

Middle Eastern Roasted Chickpeas

Servings: 3

Cooking Time: 30 Minutes

Ingredients:

- 2 tsp olive oil
- 1 can chickpeas
- Salt to taste
- 1 tsp za'atar seasoning
- 1 tsp ground sumac
- ¼ tsp garlic powder
- 1 tbsp cilantro, chopped

Directions:

1. Combine salt, za'atar, sumac, and garlic powder in a bowl. Preheat air fryer to 375°F. Put half of the chickpeas in the greased frying basket. Bake for 12 minutes, shaking every 5 minutes until crunchy and golden brown. Transfer the chickpeas to a bowl. Lightly coat them with olive oil, then toss them with half of the spice mix while they are still hot. Serve topped with cilantro.

Grilled Ham & Muenster Cheese On Raisin Bread

Servings: 1

Cooking Time: 10 Minutes

Ingredients:

- 2 slices raisin bread
- 2 tablespoons butter, softened
- 2 teaspoons honey mustard

- 3 slices thinly sliced honey ham (about 3 ounces)
- 4 slices Muenster cheese (about 3 ounces)
- 2 toothpicks

Directions:

1. Preheat the air fryer to 370°F.
2. Spread the softened butter on one side of both slices of raisin bread and place the bread, buttered side down on the counter. Spread the honey mustard on the other side of each slice of bread. Layer 2 slices of cheese, the ham and the remaining 2 slices of cheese on one slice of bread and top with the other slice of bread. Remember to leave the buttered side of the bread on the outside.
3. Transfer the sandwich to the air fryer basket and secure the sandwich with toothpicks.
4. Air-fry at 370°F for 5 minutes. Flip the sandwich over, remove the toothpicks and air-fry for another 5 minutes. Cut the sandwich in half and enjoy!!

Kale Chips

Servings: 2

Cooking Time: 5 Minutes

Ingredients:

- 4 Medium kale leaves, about 1 ounce each
- 2 teaspoons Olive oil
- 2 teaspoons Regular or low-sodium soy sauce or gluten-free tamari sauce

Directions:

1. Preheat the air fryer to 400°F.
2. Cut the stems from the leaves (all the stems, all the way up the leaf). Tear each leaf into three pieces. Put them in a large bowl.
3. Add the olive oil and soy or tamari sauce. Toss well to coat. You can even gently rub the leaves along the side of the bowl to get the liquids to stick to them.
4. When the machine is at temperature, put the leaf pieces in the basket in one layer. Air-fry for 5 minutes, turning and rearranging with kitchen tongs once halfway through, until the chips are dried out and crunchy. Watch carefully so they don't turn dark brown at the edges.
5. Gently pour the contents of the basket onto a wire rack. Cool for at least 5 minutes before serving. The chips can keep for up to 8 hours uncovered on the rack (provided it's not a humid day).

Chinese-style Potstickers

Servings: 6

Cooking Time: 30 Minutes

Ingredients:

- 1 cup shredded Chinese cabbage
- ¼ cup chopped shiitake mushrooms
- ¼ cup grated carrots
- 2 tbsp minced chives
- 2 garlic cloves, minced
- 2 tsp grated fresh ginger
- 12 dumpling wrappers
- 2 tsp sesame oil

Directions:

1. Preheat air fryer to 370°F. Toss the Chinese cabbage, shiitake mushrooms, carrots, chives, garlic, and ginger in a baking pan and stir. Place the pan in the fryer and Bake for 3-6 minutes. Put a dumpling wrapper on a clean workspace, then top with a tablespoon of the veggie mix.
2. Fold the wrapper in half to form a half-circle and use water to seal the edges. Repeat with remaining wrappers and filling. Brush the potstickers with sesame oil and arrange them on the frying basket. Air Fry for 5 minutes until the bottoms should are golden brown. Take the pan out, add 1 tbsp of water, and put it back in the fryer to Air Fry for 4-6 minutes longer. Serve hot.

Cheese Straws

Servings: 8

Cooking Time: 7 Minutes

Ingredients:

- For dusting All-purpose flour
- Two quarters of one thawed sheet (that is, a half of the sheet cut into two even pieces; wrap and re-freeze the remainder) A 17.25-ounce box frozen puff pastry
- 1 Large egg(s)
- 2 tablespoons Water
- ¼ cup (about ¾ ounce) Finely grated Parmesan cheese
- up to 1 teaspoon Ground black pepper

Directions:

1. Preheat the air fryer to 400°F.
2. Dust a clean, dry work surface with flour. Set one of the pieces of puff pastry on top, dust the pastry lightly with flour, and roll with a rolling pin to a 6-inch square.
3. Whisk the egg(s) and water in a small or medium bowl until uniform. Brush the pastry square(s) generously with this mixture. Sprinkle each square with 2 tablespoons grated cheese and up to ½ teaspoon ground black pepper.
4. Cut each square into 4 even strips. Grasp each end of 1 strip with clean, dry hands; twist it into a cheese straw. Place the twisted straws on a baking sheet.
5. Lay as many straws as will fit in the air-fryer basket—as a general rule, 4 of them in a small machine, 5 in a medium model, or 6 in a large. There should be space for air to circulate around the straws. Set the baking sheet with any remaining straws in the fridge.
6. Air-fry undisturbed for 7 minutes, or until puffed and crisp. Use tongs to transfer the cheese straws to a wire rack, then make subsequent batches in the same way (keeping the baking sheet with the remaining straws in the fridge as each batch cooks). Serve warm.

Cheese Wafers

Servings: 4

Cooking Time: 6 Minutes Per Batch

Ingredients:

- 4 ounces sharp Cheddar cheese, grated
- ¼ cup butter
- ½ cup flour
- ¼ teaspoon salt

- ½ cup crisp rice cereal
- oil for misting or cooking spray

Directions:

1. Cream the butter and grated cheese together. You can do it by hand, but using a stand mixer is faster and easier.
2. Sift flour and salt together. Add it to the cheese mixture and mix until well blended.
3. Stir in cereal.
4. Place dough on wax paper and shape into a long roll about 1 inch in diameter. Wrap well with the wax paper and chill for at least 4 hours.
5. When ready to cook, preheat air fryer to 360°F.
6. Cut cheese roll into ¼-inch slices.
7. Spray air fryer basket with oil or cooking spray and place slices in a single layer, close but not touching.
8. Cook for 6 minutes or until golden brown. When done, place them on paper towels to cool.
9. Repeat previous step to cook remaining cheese bites.

Polenta Fries With Chili-lime Mayo

Servings: 4

Cooking Time: 28 Minutes

Ingredients:

- 2 teaspoons vegetable or olive oil
- ¼ teaspoon paprika
- 1 pound prepared polenta, cut into 3-inch x ½-inch sticks
- salt and freshly ground black pepper
- Chili-Lime Mayo
- ½ cup mayonnaise
- 1 teaspoon chili powder
- ¼ teaspoon ground cumin
- juice of half a lime
- 1 teaspoon chopped fresh cilantro
- salt and freshly ground black pepper

Directions:

1. Preheat the air fryer to 400°F.
2. Combine the oil and paprika and then carefully toss the polenta sticks in the mixture.
3. Air-fry the polenta fries at 400°F for 15 minutes. Gently shake the basket to rotate the fries and continue to air-fry for another 13 minutes or until the fries have browned nicely. Season to taste with salt and freshly ground black pepper.
4. To make the chili-lime mayo, combine all the ingredients in a small bowl and stir well.
5. Serve the polenta fries warm with chili-lime mayo on the side for dipping.

Garlic Breadsticks

Servings: 12

Cooking Time: 7 Minutes

Ingredients:

- 1½ tablespoons Olive oil

- 1½ teaspoons Minced garlic
- ¼ teaspoon Table salt
- ¼ teaspoon Ground black pepper
- 6 ounces Purchased pizza dough (vegan dough, if that's a concern)

Directions:
1. Preheat the air fryer to 400°F. Mix the oil, garlic, salt, and pepper in a small bowl.
2. Divide the pizza dough into 4 balls for a small air fryer, 6 for a medium machine, or 8 for a large, each ball about the size of a walnut in its shell. (Each should weigh 1 ounce, if you want to drag out a scale and get obsessive.) Roll each ball into a 5-inch-long stick under your clean palms on a clean, dry work surface. Brush the sticks with the oil mixture.
3. When the machine is at temperature, place the prepared dough sticks in the basket, leaving a 1-inch space between them. Air-fry undisturbed for 7 minutes, or until puffed, golden, and set to the touch.
4. Use kitchen tongs to gently transfer the breadsticks to a wire rack and repeat step 3 with the remaining dough sticks.

Poultry Recipes

Fiery Chicken Meatballs

Servings: 4

Cooking Time: 20 Minutes + Chilling Time

Ingredients:

- 2 jalapeños, seeded and diced
- 2 tbsp shredded Cheddar cheese
- 1 tsp Quick Pickled Jalapeños
- 2 tbsp white wine vinegar
- ½ tsp granulated sugar
- Salt and pepper to taste
- 1 tbsp ricotta cheese
- ¾ lb ground chicken
- ¼ tsp smoked paprika
- 1 tsp garlic powder
- 1 cup bread crumbs
- ¼ tsp salt

Directions:
1. Combine the jalapeños, white wine vinegar, sugar, black pepper, and salt in a bowl. Let sit the jalapeño mixture in the fridge for 15 minutes. In a bowl, combine ricotta cheese, cheddar cheese, and 1 tsp of the jalapeños. Form mixture into 8 balls. Mix the ground chicken, smoked paprika, garlic powder, and salt in a bowl. Form mixture into 8 meatballs. Form a hole in the chicken meatballs, press a cheese ball into the hole and form chicken around the cheese ball, sealing the cheese ball in meatballs.
2. Preheat air fryer at 350ºF. Mix the breadcrumbs and salt in a bowl. Roll stuffed meatballs in the mixture.

Place the meatballs in the greased frying basket. Air Fry for 10 minutes, turning once. Serve immediately.

Intense Buffalo Chicken Wings

Servings: 2

Cooking Time: 40 Minutes

Ingredients:

- 8 chicken wings
- ½ cup melted butter
- 2 tbsp Tabasco sauce
- ½ tbsp lemon juice
- 1 tbsp Worcestershire sauce
- 2 tsp cayenne pepper
- 1 tsp garlic powder
- 1 tsp lemon zest
- Salt and pepper to taste

Directions:

1. Preheat air fryer to 350°F. Place the melted butter, Tabasco, lemon juice, Worcestershire sauce, cayenne, garlic powder, lemon zest, salt, and pepper in a bowl and stir to combine. Dip the chicken wings into the mixture, coating thoroughly. Lay the coated chicken wings on the foil-lined frying basket in an even layer. Air Fry for 16-18 minutes. Shake the basket several times during cooking until the chicken wings are crispy brown. Serve.

Philly Chicken Cheesesteak Stromboli

Servings: 2

Cooking Time: 28 Minutes

Ingredients:

- ½ onion, sliced
- 1 teaspoon vegetable oil
- 2 boneless, skinless chicken breasts, partially frozen and sliced very thin on the bias (about 1 pound)
- 1 tablespoon Worcestershire sauce
- salt and freshly ground black pepper
- ½ recipe of Blue Jean Chef pizza dough (see page 229), or 14 ounces of store-bought pizza dough
- 1½ cups grated Cheddar cheese
- ½ cup Cheese Whiz® (or other jarred cheese sauce), warmed gently in the microwave
- tomato ketchup for serving

Directions:

1. Preheat the air fryer to 400°F.
2. Toss the sliced onion with oil and air-fry for 8 minutes, stirring halfway through the cooking time. Add the sliced chicken and Worcestershire sauce to the air fryer basket, and toss to evenly distribute the ingredients. Season the mixture with salt and freshly ground black pepper and air-fry for 8 minutes, stirring a couple of times during the cooking process. Remove the chicken and onion from the air fryer and let the mixture cool a little.
3. On a lightly floured surface, roll or press the pizza dough out into a 13-inch by 11-inch rectangle, with the long side closest to you. Sprinkle half of the Cheddar cheese over the dough leaving an empty 1-inch border

from the edge farthest away from you. Top the cheese with the chicken and onion mixture, spreading it out evenly. Drizzle the cheese sauce over the meat and sprinkle the remaining Cheddar cheese on top.
4. Start rolling the stromboli away from you and toward the empty border. Make sure the filling stays tightly tucked inside the roll. Finally, tuck the ends of the dough in and pinch the seam shut. Place the seam side down and shape the Stromboli into a U-shape to fit in the air-fry basket. Cut 4 small slits with the tip of a sharp knife evenly in the top of the dough and lightly brush the stromboli with a little oil.
5. Preheat the air fryer to 370°F.
6. Spray or brush the air fryer basket with oil and transfer the U-shaped stromboli to the air fryer basket. Air-fry for 12 minutes, turning the stromboli over halfway through the cooking time. (Use a plate to invert the stromboli out of the air fryer basket and then slide it back into the basket off the plate.)
7. To remove, carefully flip stromboli over onto a cutting board. Let it rest for a couple of minutes before serving. Slice the stromboli into 3-inch pieces and serve with ketchup for dipping, if desired.

Farmer's Fried Chicken

Servings: 4

Cooking Time: 55 Minutes

Ingredients:

- 3 lb whole chicken, cut into breasts, drumsticks, and thighs
- 2 cups flour
- 4 tsp salt
- 4 tsp dried basil
- 4 tsp dried thyme
- 2 tsp dried shallot powder
- 2 tsp smoked paprika
- 1 tsp mustard powder
- 1 tsp celery salt
- 1 cup kefir
- ¼ cup honey

Directions:

1. Preheat the air fryer to 370°F. Combine the flour, salt, basil, thyme, shallot, paprika, mustard powder, and celery salt in a bowl. Pour into a glass jar. Mix the kefir and honey in a large bowl and add the chicken, stir to coat. Marinate for 15 minutes at room temperature. Remove the chicken from the kefir mixture; discard the rest. Put 2/3 cup of the flour mix onto a plate and dip the chicken. Shake gently and put on a wire rack for 10 minutes. Line the frying basket with round parchment paper with holes punched in it. Place the chicken in a single layer and spray with cooking oil. Air Fry for 18-25 minutes, flipping once around minute 10. Serve hot.

Crispy "fried" Chicken

Servings: 4

Cooking Time: 14 Minutes

Ingredients:

- ¾ cup all-purpose flour
- ½ teaspoon paprika
- ¼ teaspoon black pepper
- ¼ teaspoon salt

- 2 large eggs
- 1½ cups panko breadcrumbs
- 1 pound boneless, skinless chicken tenders

Directions:

1. Preheat the air fryer to 400°F.
2. In a shallow bowl, mix the flour with the paprika, pepper, and salt.
3. In a separate bowl, whisk the eggs; set aside.
4. In a third bowl, place the breadcrumbs.
5. Liberally spray the air fryer basket with olive oil spray.
6. Pat the chicken tenders dry with a paper towel. Dredge the tenders one at a time in the flour, then dip them in the egg, and toss them in the breadcrumb coating. Repeat until all tenders are coated.
7. Set each tender in the air fryer, leaving room on each side of the tender to allow for flipping.
8. When the basket is full, cook 4 to 7 minutes, flip, and cook another 4 to 7 minutes.
9. Remove the tenders and let cool 5 minutes before serving. Repeat until all tenders are cooked.

Buttered Chicken Thighs

Servings: 4

Cooking Time: 30 Minutes

Ingredients:

- 4 bone-in chicken thighs, skinless
- 2 tbsp butter, melted
- 1 tsp garlic powder
- 1 tsp lemon zest
- Salt and pepper to taste
- 1 lemon, sliced

Directions:

1. Preheat air fryer to 380°F. Stir the chicken thighs in the butter, lemon zest, garlic powder, and salt. Divide the chicken thighs between 4 pieces of foil and sprinkle with black pepper, and then top with slices of lemon. Bake in the air fryer for 20-22 minutes until golden. Serve.

Yummy Maple-mustard Chicken Kabobs

Servings: 4

Cooking Time: 35 Minutes+ Chilling Time

Ingredients:

- 1 lb boneless, skinless chicken thighs, cubed
- 1 green bell pepper, chopped
- ½ cup honey mustard
- ½ yellow onion, chopped
- 8 cherry tomatoes
- 2 tbsp chopped scallions

Directions:

1. Toss chicken cubes and honey mustard in a bowl and let chill covered in the fridge for 30 minutes. Preheat air fryer to 350ºF. Thread chicken cubes, onion, cherry tomatoes, and bell peppers, alternating, onto 8 skewers. Place them on a kebab rack. Place rack in the frying basket and Air Fry for 12 minutes. Top with scallions to

serve.

Sunday Chicken Skewers

Servings: 4

Cooking Time: 25 Minutes

Ingredients:

- 1 green bell pepper, cut into chunks
- 1 red bell pepper, cut into chunks
- 4 chicken breasts, cubed
- 1 tbsp chicken seasoning
- Salt and pepper to taste
- 16 cherry tomatoes
- 8 pearl onions, peeled

Directions:

1. Preheat air fryer to 360°F. Season the cubes with chicken seasoning, salt, and pepper. Thread metal skewers with chicken, bell pepper chunks, cherry tomatoes, and pearl onions. Put the kabobs in the greased frying basket. Bake for 14-16 minutes, flipping once until cooked through. Let cool slightly. Serve.

Teriyaki Chicken Bites

Servings: 4

Cooking Time: 30 Minutes

Ingredients:

- 1 lb boneless, skinless chicken thighs, cubed
- 1 green onion, sliced diagonally
- 1 large egg
- 1 tbsp teriyaki sauce
- 4 tbsp flour
- 1 tsp sesame oil
- 2 tsp balsamic vinegar
- 2 tbsp tamari
- 3 cloves garlic, minced
- 2 tsp grated fresh ginger
- 2 tsp chili garlic sauce
- 2 tsp granular honey
- Salt and pepper to taste

Directions:

1. Preheat air fryer to 400°F. Beat the egg, teriyaki sauce, and flour in a bowl. Stir in chicken pieces until fully coated. In another bowl, combine the remaining ingredients, except for the green onion. Reserve. Place chicken pieces in the frying basket lightly greased with olive oil and Air Fry for 15 minutes, tossing every 5 minutes. Remove them to the bowl with the sauce and toss to coat. Scatter with green onions to serve. Enjoy!

Country Chicken Hoagies

Servings: 2

Cooking Time: 30 Minutes

Ingredients:

- ¼ cup button mushrooms, sliced
- 1 hoagie bun, halved
- 1 chicken breast, cubed
- ½ white onion, sliced
- 1 cup bell pepper strips
- 2 cheddar cheese slices

Directions:

1. Preheat air fryer to 320°F. Place the chicken pieces, onions, bell pepper strips, and mushroom slices on one side of the frying basket. Lay the hoagie bun halves, crusty side up and soft side down, on the other half of the air fryer. Bake for 10 minutes. Flip the hoagie buns and cover with cheddar cheese. Stir the chicken and vegetables. Cook for another 6 minutes until the cheese is melted and the chicken is juicy on the inside and crispy on the outside. Place the cheesy hoagie halves on a serving plate and cover one half with the chicken and veggies. Close with the other cheesy hoagie half. Serve.

Maple Bacon Wrapped Chicken Breasts

Servings: 2

Cooking Time: 18 Minutes

Ingredients:

- 2 (6-ounce) boneless, skinless chicken breasts
- 2 tablespoons maple syrup, divided
- freshly ground black pepper
- 6 slices thick-sliced bacon
- fresh celery or parsley leaves
- Ranch Dressing:
- ¼ cup mayonnaise
- ¼ cup buttermilk
- ¼ cup Greek yogurt
- 1 tablespoon chopped fresh chives
- 1 tablespoon chopped fresh parsley
- 1 tablespoon chopped fresh dill
- 1 tablespoon lemon juice
- salt and freshly ground black pepper

Directions:

1. Brush the chicken breasts with half the maple syrup and season with freshly ground black pepper. Wrap three slices of bacon around each chicken breast, securing the ends with toothpicks.
2. Preheat the air fryer to 380°F.
3. Air-fry the chicken for 6 minutes. Then turn the chicken breasts over, pour more maple syrup on top and air-fry for another 6 minutes. Turn the chicken breasts one more time, brush the remaining maple syrup all over and continue to air-fry for a final 6 minutes.
4. While the chicken is cooking, prepare the dressing by combining all the dressing ingredients together in a

bowl.

5. When the chicken has finished cooking, remove the toothpicks and serve each breast with a little dressing drizzled over each one. Scatter lots of fresh celery or parsley leaves on top.

Glazed Chicken Thighs

Servings: 4

Cooking Time: 25 Minutes

Ingredients:

- 1 lb boneless, skinless chicken thighs
- ¼ cup balsamic vinegar
- 3 tbsp honey
- 2 tbsp brown sugar
- 1 tsp whole-grain mustard
- ¼ cup soy sauce
- 3 garlic cloves, minced
- Salt and pepper to taste
- ½ tsp smoked paprika
- 2 tbsp chopped shallots

Directions:

1. Preheat air fryer to 375°F. Whisk vinegar, honey, sugar, soy sauce, mustard, garlic, salt, pepper, and paprika in a small bowl. Arrange the chicken in the frying basket and brush the top of each with some of the vinegar mixture. Air Fry for 7 minutes, then flip the chicken. Brush the tops with the rest of the vinegar mixture and Air Fry for another 5 to 8 minutes. Allow resting for 5 minutes before slicing. Serve warm sprinkled with shallots.

Chicken Meatballs With A Surprise

Servings: 4

Cooking Time: 35 Minutes

Ingredients:

- 1/3 cup cottage cheese crumbles
- 1 lb ground chicken
- ½ tsp onion powder
- ¼ cup chopped basil
- ½ cup bread crumbs
- ½ tsp garlic powder

Directions:

1. Preheat air fryer to 350ºF. Combine the ground chicken, onion, basil, cottage cheese, bread crumbs, and garlic powder in a bowl. Form into 18 meatballs, about 2 tbsp each. Place the chicken meatballs in the greased frying basket and Air Fry for 12 minutes, shaking once. Serve.

Spicy Black Bean Turkey Burgers With Cumin-avocado Spread

Servings: 2

Cooking Time: 20 Minutes

Ingredients:

- 1 cup canned black beans, drained and rinsed
- ¾ pound lean ground turkey
- 2 tablespoons minced red onion
- 1 Jalapeño pepper, seeded and minced
- 2 tablespoons plain breadcrumbs
- ½ teaspoon chili powder
- ¼ teaspoon cayenne pepper
- salt, to taste
- olive or vegetable oil
- 2 slices pepper jack cheese
- toasted burger rolls, sliced tomatoes, lettuce leaves
- Cumin-Avocado Spread:
- 1 ripe avocado
- juice of 1 lime
- 1 teaspoon ground cumin
- ½ teaspoon salt
- 1 tablespoon chopped fresh cilantro
- freshly ground black pepper

Directions:

1. Place the black beans in a large bowl and smash them slightly with the back of a fork. Add the ground turkey, red onion, Jalapeño pepper, breadcrumbs, chili powder and cayenne pepper. Season with salt. Mix with your hands to combine all the ingredients and then shape them into 2 patties. Brush both sides of the burger patties with a little olive or vegetable oil.
2. Preheat the air fryer to 380°F.
3. Transfer the burgers to the air fryer basket and air-fry for 20 minutes, flipping them over halfway through the cooking process. Top the burgers with the pepper jack cheese (securing the slices to the burgers with a toothpick) for the last 2 minutes of the cooking process.
4. While the burgers are cooking, make the cumin avocado spread. Place the avocado, lime juice, cumin and salt in food processor and process until smooth. (For a chunkier spread, you can mash this by hand in a bowl.) Stir in the cilantro and season with freshly ground black pepper. Chill the spread until you are ready to serve.
5. When the burgers have finished cooking, remove them from the air fryer and let them rest on a plate, covered gently with aluminum foil. Brush a little olive oil on the insides of the burger rolls. Place the rolls, cut side up, into the air fryer basket and air-fry at 400°F for 1 minute to toast and warm them.
6. Spread the cumin-avocado spread on the rolls and build your burgers with lettuce and sliced tomatoes and any other ingredient you like. Serve warm with a side of sweet potato fries.

Poblano Bake

Servings: 4

Cooking Time: 11 Minutes Per Batch

Ingredients:

- 2 large poblano peppers (approx. 5½ inches long excluding stem)
- ¾ pound ground turkey, raw
- ¾ cup cooked brown rice
- 1 teaspoon chile powder

- ½ teaspoon ground cumin
- ½ teaspoon garlic powder
- 4 ounces sharp Cheddar cheese, grated
- 1 8-ounce jar salsa, warmed

Directions:

1. Slice each pepper in half lengthwise so that you have four wide, flat pepper halves.
2. Remove seeds and membrane and discard. Rinse inside and out.
3. In a large bowl, combine turkey, rice, chile powder, cumin, and garlic powder. Mix well.
4. Divide turkey filling into 4 portions and stuff one into each of the 4 pepper halves. Press lightly to pack down.
5. Place 2 pepper halves in air fryer basket and cook at 390°F for 10minutes or until turkey is well done.
6. Top each pepper half with ¼ of the grated cheese. Cook 1 more minute or just until cheese melts.
7. Repeat steps 5 and 6 to cook remaining pepper halves.
8. To serve, place each pepper half on a plate and top with ¼ cup warm salsa.

Punjabi-inspired Chicken

Servings: 4

Cooking Time: 35 Minutes

Ingredients:

- 2/3 cup plain yogurt
- 2 tbsp lemon juice
- 2 tsp curry powder
- ½ tsp ground cinnamon
- 2 garlic cloves, minced
- ½-inch piece ginger, grated
- 2 tsp olive oil
- 4 chicken breasts

Directions:

1. Mix the yogurt, lemon juice, curry powder, cinnamon, garlic, ginger, and olive oil in a bowl. Slice the chicken, without cutting, all the way through, by making thin slits, then toss it into the yogurt mix. Coat well and let marinate for 10 minutes.
2. Preheat air fryer to 360°F. Take the chicken out of the marinade, letting the extra liquid drip off. Toss the rest of the marinade away. Air Fry the chicken for 10 minutes. Turn each piece, then cook for 8-13 minutes more until cooked through and no pink meat remains. Serve warm.

Buttered Turkey Breasts

Servings: 6

Cooking Time: 65 Minutes

Ingredients:

- ½ cup butter, melted
- 6 garlic cloves, minced
- 1 tsp dried oregano
- ½ tsp dried thyme
- ½ tsp dried rosemary
- Salt and pepper to taste

- 4 lb bone-in turkey breast
- 1 tbsp chopped cilantro

Directions:

1. Preheat air fryer to 350°F. Combine butter, garlic, oregano, salt, and pepper in a small bowl. Place the turkey breast on a plate and coat the entire turkey with the butter mixture. Put the turkey breast-side down in the frying basket and scatter with thyme and rosemary. Bake for 20 minutes. Flip the turkey so that the breast side is up, then bake for another 20-30 minutes until it has an internal temperature of 165°F. Allow to rest for 10 minutes before carving. Serve sprinkled with cilantro.

Harissa Chicken Wings

Servings: 4

Cooking Time: 25 Minutes

Ingredients:

- 8 whole chicken wings
- 1 tsp garlic powder
- ¼ tsp dried oregano
- 1 tbsp harissa seasoning

Directions:

1. Preheat air fryer to 400°F. Season the wings with garlic, harissa seasoning, and oregano. Place them in the greased frying basket and spray with cooking oil spray. Air Fry for 10 minutes, shake the basket, and cook for another 5-7 minutes until golden and crispy. Serve warm.

Cajun Chicken Livers

Servings: 2

Cooking Time: 45 Minutes

Ingredients:

- 1 lb chicken livers, rinsed, connective tissue discarded
- 1 cup whole milk
- ½ cup cornmeal
- 3/4 cup flour
- 1 tsp salt and black pepper
- 1 tsp Cajun seasoning
- 2 eggs
- 1 ½ cups bread crumbs
- 1 tbsp olive oil
- 2 tbsp chopped parsley

Directions:

1. Pat chicken livers dry with paper towels, then transfer them to a small bowl and pour in the milk and black pepper. Let sit covered in the fridge for 2 hours.
2. Preheat air fryer at 375°F. In a bowl, combine cornmeal, flour, salt, and Cajun seasoning. In another bowl, beat the eggs, and in a third bowl, add bread crumbs. Dip chicken livers first in the cornmeal mixture, then in the egg, and finally in the bread crumbs. Place chicken livers in the greased frying basket, brush the tops lightly with olive oil, and Air Fry for 16 minutes, turning once. Serve right away sprinkled with parsley.

Basic Chicken Breasts(1)

Servings: 4

Cooking Time: 15 Minutes

Ingredients:

- 2 tsp olive oil
- 4 chicken breasts
- Salt and pepper to taste
- 1 tbsp Italian seasoning

Directions:

1. Preheat air fryer at 350ºF. Rub olive oil over chicken breasts and sprinkle with salt, Italian seasoning and black pepper. Place them in the frying basket and Air Fry for 8-10 minutes. Let rest for 5 minutes before cutting. Store it covered in the fridge for up to 1 week.

Beef, pork & Lamb Recipes

Sweet Potato-crusted Pork Rib Chops

Servings: 2

Cooking Time: 14 Minutes

Ingredients:

- 2 Large egg white(s), well beaten
- 1½ cups (about 6 ounces) Crushed sweet potato chips (certified gluten-free, if a concern)
- 1 teaspoon Ground cinnamon
- 1 teaspoon Ground dried ginger
- 1 teaspoon Table salt (optional)
- 2 10-ounce, 1-inch-thick bone-in pork rib chop(s)

Directions:

1. Preheat the air fryer to 375°F.
2. Set up and fill two shallow soup plates or small pie plates on your counter: one for the beaten egg white(s); and one for the crushed chips, mixed with the cinnamon, ginger, and salt (if using).
3. Dip a chop in the egg white(s), coating it on both sides as well as the edges. Let the excess egg white slip back into the rest, then set it in the crushed chip mixture. Turn it several times, pressing gently, until evenly coated on both sides and the edges. If necessary, set the chop aside and coat the remaining chop(s).
4. Set the chop(s) in the basket with as much air space between them as possible. Air-fry undisturbed for 12 minutes, or until crunchy and browned and an instant-read meat thermometer inserted into the center of a chop (without touching bone) registers 145°F. If the machine is at 360°F, you may need to add 2 minutes to the cooking time.
5. Use kitchen tongs to transfer the chop(s) to a wire rack. Cool for 2 or 3 minutes before serving.

Meat Loaves

Servings: 4

Cooking Time: 19 Minutes

Ingredients:

- Sauce
- ¼ cup white vinegar
- ¼ cup brown sugar
- 2 tablespoons Worcestershire sauce
- ½ cup ketchup
- Meat Loaves
- 1 pound very lean ground beef
- ⅔ cup dry bread (approx. 1 slice torn into small pieces)
- 1 egg
- ⅓ cup minced onion
- 1 teaspoon salt
- 2 tablespoons ketchup

Directions:

1. In a small saucepan, combine all sauce ingredients and bring to a boil. Remove from heat and stir to ensure that brown sugar dissolves completely.
2. In a large bowl, combine the beef, bread, egg, onion, salt, and ketchup. Mix well.
3. Divide meat mixture into 4 portions and shape each into a thick, round patty. Patties will be about 3 to 3½ inches in diameter, and all four should fit easily into the air fryer basket at once.
4. Cook at 360°F for 18 minutes, until meat is well done. Baste tops of mini loaves with a small amount of sauce, and cook 1 minute.
5. Serve hot with additional sauce on the side.

Skirt Steak Fajitas

Servings: 4

Cooking Time: 30 Minutes

Ingredients:

- 2 tablespoons olive oil
- ¼ cup lime juice
- 1 clove garlic, minced
- ½ teaspoon ground cumin
- ½ teaspoon hot sauce
- ½ teaspoon salt
- 2 tablespoons chopped fresh cilantro
- 1 pound skirt steak
- 1 onion, sliced
- 1 teaspoon chili powder
- 1 red pepper, sliced
- 1 green pepper, sliced
- salt and freshly ground black pepper
- 8 flour tortillas

- shredded lettuce, crumbled Queso Fresco (or grated Cheddar cheese), sliced black olives, diced tomatoes, sour cream and guacamole for serving

Directions:

1. Combine the olive oil, lime juice, garlic, cumin, hot sauce, salt and cilantro in a shallow dish. Add the skirt steak and turn it over several times to coat all sides. Pierce the steak with a needle-style meat tenderizer or paring knife. Marinate the steak in the refrigerator for at least 3 hours, or overnight. When you are ready to cook, remove the steak from the refrigerator and let it sit at room temperature for 30 minutes.
2. Preheat the air fryer to 400°F.
3. Toss the onion slices with the chili powder and a little olive oil and transfer them to the air fryer basket. Air-fry at 400°F for 5 minutes. Add the red and green peppers to the air fryer basket with the onions, season with salt and pepper and air-fry for 8 more minutes, until the onions and peppers are soft. Transfer the vegetables to a dish and cover with aluminum foil to keep warm.
4. Place the skirt steak in the air fryer basket and pour the marinade over the top. Air-fry at 400°F for 12 minutes. Flip the steak over and air-fry at 400°F for an additional 5 minutes. (The time needed for your steak will depend on the thickness of the skirt steak. 17 minutes should bring your steak to roughly medium.) Transfer the cooked steak to a cutting board and let the steak rest for a few minutes. If the peppers and onions need to be heated, return them to the air fryer for just 1 to 2 minutes.
5. Thinly slice the steak at an angle, cutting against the grain of the steak. Serve the steak with the onions and peppers, the warm tortillas and the fajita toppings on the side so that everyone can make their own fajita.

Sirloin Steak Flatbread

Servings: 2

Cooking Time: 40 Minutes

Ingredients:

- 1 premade flatbread dough
- 1 sirloin steak, cubed
- 2 cups breadcrumbs
- 2 eggs, beaten
- Salt and pepper to taste
- 2 tsp onion powder
- 1 tsp garlic powder
- 1 tsp dried thyme
- ½ onion, sliced
- 2 Swiss cheese slices

Directions:

1. Preheat air fryer to 360°F. Place the breadcrumbs, onion powder, garlic powder, thyme, salt, and pepper in a bowl and stir to combine. Add in the steak cubes, coating all sides. Dip into the beaten eggs, then dip again into the crumbs. Lay the coated steak pieces on half of the greased fryer basket. Place the onion slices on the other half of the basket. Air Fry 6 minutes. Turn the onions over and flip the steak pieces. Continue cooking for another 6 minutes. Roll the flatbread out and pierce it several times with a fork. Cover with Swiss cheese slices.
2. When the steak and onions are ready, remove them to the cheese-covered flatbread dough. Fold the flatbread over. Arrange the folded flatbread on the frying basket. Bake for 10 minutes, flipping once until golden brown. Serve.

Chinese-style Lamb Chops

Servings: 4

Cooking Time: 25 Minutes

Ingredients:

- 8 lamb chops, trimmed
- 2 tbsp scallions, sliced
- ¼ tsp Chinese five-spice
- 3 garlic cloves, crushed
- ½ tsp ginger powder
- ¼ cup dark soy sauce
- 2 tsp orange juice
- 3 tbsp honey
- ½ tbsp light brown sugar
- ¼ tsp red pepper flakes

Directions:

1. Season the chops with garlic, ginger, soy sauce, five-spice powder, orange juice, and honey in a bowl. Toss to coat. Cover the bowl with plastic wrap and marinate for 2 hours and up to overnight.
2. Preheat air fryer to 400°F. Remove the chops from the bowl but reserve the marinade. Place the chops in the greased frying basket and Bake for 5 minutes. Using tongs, flip the chops. Brush the lamb with the reserved marinade, then sprinkle with brown sugar and pepper flakes. Cook for another 4 minutes until brown and caramelized medium-rare. Serve with scallions on top.

Beef Al Carbon (street Taco Meat)

Servings: 6

Cooking Time: 8 Minutes

Ingredients:

- 1½ pounds sirloin steak, cut into ½-inch cubes
- ¾ cup lime juice
- ½ cup extra-virgin olive oil
- 1 teaspoon ground cumin
- 2 teaspoons garlic powder
- 1 teaspoon salt

Directions:

1. In a large bowl, toss together the steak, lime juice, olive oil, cumin, garlic powder, and salt. Allow the meat to marinate for 30 minutes. Drain off all the marinade and pat the meat dry with paper towels.
2. Preheat the air fryer to 400°F.
3. Place the meat in the air fryer basket and spray with cooking spray. Cook the meat for 5 minutes, toss the meat, and continue cooking another 3 minutes, until slightly crispy.

Indonesian Pork Satay

Servings: 4

Cooking Time: 30 Minutes

Ingredients:

- 1 lb pork tenderloin, cubed
- ¼ cup minced onion
- 2 garlic cloves, minced
- 1 jalapeño pepper, minced
- 2 tbsp lime juice
- 2 tbsp coconut milk
- ½ tbsp ground coriander
- ½ tsp ground cumin
- 2 tbsp peanut butter
- 2 tsp curry powder

Directions:

1. Combine the pork, onion, garlic, jalapeño, lime juice, coconut milk, peanut butter, ground coriander, cumin, and curry powder in a bowl. Stir well and allow to marinate for 10 minutes.
2. Preheat air fryer to 380°F. Use a holey spoon and take the pork out of the marinade and set the marinade aside. Poke 8 bamboo skewers through the meat, then place the skewers in the air fryer. Use a cooking brush to rub the marinade on each skewer, then Grill for 10-14 minutes, adding more marinade if necessary. The pork should be golden and cooked through when finished. Serve warm.

Balsamic Marinated Rib Eye Steak With Balsamic Fried Cipollini Onions

Servings: 2

Cooking Time: 22-26 Minutes

Ingredients:

- 3 tablespoons balsamic vinegar
- 2 cloves garlic, sliced
- 1 tablespoon Dijon mustard
- 1 teaspoon fresh thyme leaves
- 1 (16-ounce) boneless rib eye steak
- coarsely ground black pepper
- salt
- 1 (8-ounce) bag cipollini onions, peeled
- 1 teaspoon balsamic vinegar

Directions:

1. Combine the 3 tablespoons of balsamic vinegar, garlic, Dijon mustard and thyme in a small bowl. Pour this marinade over the steak. Pierce the steak several times with a paring knife or
2. a needle-style meat tenderizer and season it generously with coarsely ground black pepper. Flip the steak over and pierce the other side in a similar fashion, seasoning again with the coarsely ground black pepper. Marinate the steak for 2 to 24 hours in the refrigerator. When you are ready to cook, remove the steak from the refrigerator and let it sit at room temperature for 30 minutes.
3. Preheat the air fryer to 400°F.
4. Season the steak with salt and air-fry at 400°F for 12 minutes (medium-rare), 14 minutes (medium), or 16 minutes (well-done), flipping the steak once half way through the cooking time.
5. While the steak is air-frying, toss the onions with 1 teaspoon of balsamic vinegar and season with salt.
6. Remove the steak from the air fryer and let it rest while you fry the onions. Transfer the onions to the air fryer basket and air-fry for 10 minutes, adding a few more minutes if your onions are very large. Then, slice the

steak on the bias and serve with the fried onions on top.

Stress-free Beef Patties

Servings: 2

Cooking Time: 30 Minutes

Ingredients:

- ½ lb ground beef
- 1 ½ tbsp ketchup
- 1 ½ tbsp tamari
- ½ tsp jalapeño powder
- ½ tsp mustard powder
- Salt and pepper to taste

Directions:

1. Preheat air fryer to 350°F. Add the beef, ketchup, tamari, jalapeño, mustard salt, and pepper in a bowl and mix until evenly combined. Shape into 2 patties, then place them on the greased frying basket. Air Fry for 18-20 minutes, turning once. Serve and enjoy!

Steakhouse Burgers With Red Onion Compote

Servings: 4

Cooking Time: 22 Minutes

Ingredients:

- 1½ pounds lean ground beef
- 2 cloves garlic, minced and divided
- 1 teaspoon Worcestershire sauce
- 1 teaspoon sea salt, divided
- ½ teaspoon black pepper
- 1 tablespoon extra-virgin olive oil
- 1 red onion, thinly sliced
- ¼ cup balsamic vinegar
- 1 teaspoon sugar
- 1 tablespoon tomato paste
- 2 tablespoons mayonnaise
- 2 tablespoons sour cream
- 4 brioche hamburger buns
- 1 cup arugula

Directions:

1. In a large bowl, mix together the ground beef, 1 of the minced garlic cloves, the Worcestershire sauce, ½ teaspoon of the salt, and the black pepper. Form the meat into 1-inch-thick patties. Make a dent in the center (this helps the center cook evenly). Let the meat sit for 15 minutes.
2. Meanwhile, in a small saucepan over medium heat, cook the olive oil and red onion for 4 minutes, stirring frequently to avoid burning. Add in the balsamic vinegar, sugar, and tomato paste, and cook for an additional 3 minutes, stirring frequently. Transfer the onion compote to a small bowl.
3. Preheat the air fryer to 350°F.
4. In another small bowl, mix together the remaining minced garlic, the mayonnaise, and the sour cream. Spread

the mayo mixture on the insides of the brioche buns.
5. Cook the hamburgers for 6 minutes, flip the burgers, and cook an additional 2 to 6 minutes. Check the internal temperature to avoid under- or overcooking. Hamburgers should be cooked to at least 160°F. After cooking, cover with foil and let the meat rest for 5 minutes.
6. Meanwhile, place the buns inside the air fryer and toast them for 3 minutes.
7. To assemble the burgers, place the hamburger on one side of the bun, top with onion compote and ¼ cup arugula, and then place the other half of the bun on top.

Red Curry Flank Steak

Servings: 4

Cooking Time: 18 Minutes

Ingredients:

- 3 tablespoons red curry paste
- ¼ cup olive oil
- 2 teaspoons grated fresh ginger
- 2 tablespoons soy sauce
- 2 tablespoons rice wine vinegar
- 3 scallions, minced
- 1½ pounds flank steak
- fresh cilantro (or parsley) leaves

Directions:

1. Mix the red curry paste, olive oil, ginger, soy sauce, rice vinegar and scallions together in a bowl. Place the flank steak in a shallow glass dish and pour half the marinade over the steak. Pierce the steak several times with a fork or meat tenderizer to let the marinade penetrate the meat. Turn the steak over, pour the remaining marinade over the top and pierce the steak several times again. Cover and marinate the steak in the refrigerator for 6 to 8 hours.
2. When you are ready to cook, remove the steak from the refrigerator and let it sit at room temperature for 30 minutes.
3. Preheat the air fryer to 400°F.
4. Cut the flank steak in half so that it fits more easily into the air fryer and transfer both pieces to the air fryer basket. Pour the marinade over the steak. Air-fry for 18 minutes, depending on your preferred degree of doneness of the steak (12 minutes = medium rare). Flip the steak over halfway through the cooking time.
5. When your desired degree of doneness has been reached, remove the steak to a cutting board and let it rest for 5 minutes before slicing. Thinly slice the flank steak against the grain of the meat. Transfer the slices to a serving platter, pour any juice from the bottom of the air fryer over the sliced flank steak and sprinkle the fresh cilantro on top.

Tamari-seasoned Pork Strips

Servings:4

Cooking Time: 40 Minutes

Ingredients:

- 3 tbsp olive oil
- 2 tbsp tamari
- 2 tsp red chili paste

- 2 tsp yellow mustard
- 2 tsp granulated sugar
- 1 lb pork shoulder strips
- 1 cup white rice, cooked
- 6 scallions, chopped
- ½ tsp garlic powder
- 1 tbsp lemon juice
- 1 tsp lemon zest
- ½ tsp salt

Directions:

1. Add 2 tbsp of olive oil, tamari, chili paste, mustard, and sugar to a bowl and whisk until everything is well mixed. Set aside half of the marinade. Toss pork strips in the remaining marinade and put in the fridge for 30 minutes.
2. Preheat air fryer to 350ºF. Place the pork strips in the frying basket and Air Fry for 16-18 minutes, tossing once. Transfer cooked pork to the bowl along with the remaining marinade and toss to coat. Set aside. In a medium bowl, stir in the cooked rice, garlic, lemon juice, lemon zest, and salt and cover. Spread on a serving plate. Arrange the pork strips over and top with scallions. Serve.

Easy Carnitas

Servings: 3

Cooking Time: 25 Minutes

Ingredients:

- 1½ pounds Boneless country-style pork ribs, cut into 2-inch pieces
- ¼ cup Orange juice
- 2 tablespoons Brine from a jar of pickles, any type, even pickled jalapeño rings (gluten-free, if a concern)
- 2 teaspoons Minced garlic
- 2 teaspoons Minced fresh oregano leaves
- ¾ teaspoon Ground cumin
- ¾ teaspoon Table salt
- ¾ teaspoon Ground black pepper

Directions:

1. Mix the country-style pork rib pieces, orange juice, pickle brine, garlic, oregano, cumin, salt, and pepper in a large bowl. Cover and refrigerate for at least 2 hours or up to 10 hours, stirring the mixture occasionally.
2. Preheat the air fryer to 400°F. Set the rib pieces in their bowl on the counter as the machine heats.
3. Use kitchen tongs to transfer the rib pieces to the basket, arranging them in one layer. Some may touch. Air-fry for 25 minutes, turning and rearranging the pieces at the 10- and 20-minute marks to make sure all surfaces have been exposed to the air currents, until browned and sizzling.
4. Use clean kitchen tongs to transfer the rib pieces to a wire rack. Cool for a couple of minutes before serving.

Skirt Steak With Horseradish Cream

Servings: 2

Cooking Time: 20 Minutes

Ingredients:

- 1 cup heavy cream
- 3 tbsp horseradish sauce
- 1 lemon, zested
- 1 skirt steak, halved
- 2 tbsp olive oil
- Salt and pepper to taste

Directions:

1. Mix together the heavy cream, horseradish sauce, and lemon zest in a small bowl. Let chill in the fridge.
2. Preheat air fryer to 400ºF. Brush steak halves with olive oil and sprinkle with salt and pepper. Place steaks in the frying basket and Air Fry for 10 minutes or until you reach your desired doneness, flipping once. Let sit onto a cutting board for 5 minutes. Thinly slice against the grain and divide between 2 plates. Drizzle with the horseradish sauce over. Serve and enjoy!

Kielbasa Chunks With Pineapple & Peppers

Servings: 2

Cooking Time: 10 Minutes

Ingredients:

- ¾ pound kielbasa sausage
- 1 cup bell pepper chunks (any color)
- 1 8-ounce can pineapple chunks in juice, drained
- 1 tablespoon barbeque seasoning
- 1 tablespoon soy sauce
- cooking spray

Directions:

1. Cut sausage into ½-inch slices.
2. In a medium bowl, toss all ingredients together.
3. Spray air fryer basket with nonstick cooking spray.
4. Pour sausage mixture into the basket.
5. Cook at 390°F for approximately 5minutes. Shake basket and cook an additional 5minutes.

Kochukaru Pork Lettuce Cups

Servings: 4

Cooking Time: 25 Minutes

Ingredients:

- 1 tsp kochukaru (chili pepper flakes)
- 12 baby romaine lettuce leaves
- 1 lb pork tenderloin, sliced
- Salt and pepper to taste
- 3 scallions, chopped
- 3 garlic cloves, crushed
- ¼ cup soy sauce
- 2 tbsp gochujang
- ½ tbsp light brown sugar
- ½ tbsp honey

- 1 tbsp grated fresh ginger
- 2 tbsp rice vinegar
- 1 tsp toasted sesame oil
- 2 ¼ cups cooked brown rice
- ½ tbsp sesame seeds
- 2 spring onions, sliced

Directions:

1. Mix the scallions, garlic, soy sauce, kochukaru, honey, brown sugar, and ginger in a small bowl. Mix well. Place the pork in a large bowl. Season with salt and pepper. Pour the marinade over the pork, tossing the meat in the marinade until coated. Cover the bowl with plastic wrap and allow to marinate overnight. When ready to cook,
2. Preheat air fryer to 400°F. Remove the pork from the bowl and discard the marinade. Place the pork in the greased frying basket and Air Fry for 10 minutes, flipping once until browned and cooked through. Meanwhile, prepare the gochujang sauce. Mix the gochujang, rice vinegar, and sesame oil until smooth. To make the cup, add 3 tbsp of brown rice on the lettuce leaf. Place a slice of pork on top, drizzle a tsp of gochujang sauce and sprinkle with some sesame seeds and spring onions. Wrap the lettuce over the mixture similar to a burrito. Serve warm.

Lamb Burger With Feta And Olives

Servings: 3

Cooking Time: 16 Minutes

Ingredients:

- 2 teaspoons olive oil
- ⅓ onion, finely chopped
- 1 clove garlic, minced
- 1 pound ground lamb
- 2 tablespoons fresh parsley, finely chopped
- 1½ teaspoons fresh oregano, finely chopped
- ½ cup black olives, finely chopped
- ⅓ cup crumbled feta cheese
- ½ teaspoon salt
- freshly ground black pepper
- 4 thick pita breads
- toppings and condiments

Directions:

1. Preheat a medium skillet over medium-high heat on the stovetop. Add the olive oil and cook the onion until tender, but not browned – about 4 to 5 minutes. Add the garlic and cook for another minute. Transfer the onion and garlic to a mixing bowl and add the ground lamb, parsley, oregano, olives, feta cheese, salt and pepper. Gently mix the ingredients together.
2. Divide the mixture into 3 or 4 equal portions and then form the hamburgers, being careful not to over-handle the meat. One good way to do this is to throw the meat back and forth between your hands like a baseball, packing the meat each time you catch it. Flatten the balls into patties, making an indentation in the center of each patty. Flatten the sides of the patties as well to make it easier to fit them into the air fryer basket.
3. Preheat the air fryer to 370°F.
4. If you don't have room for all four burgers, air-fry two or three burgers at a time for 8 minutes at 370°F. Flip the burgers over and air-fry for another 8 minutes. If you cooked your burgers in batches, return the first batch of burgers to the air fryer for the last two minutes of cooking to re-heat. This should give you a medi-

um-well burger. If you'd prefer a medium-rare burger, shorten the cooking time to about 13 minutes. Remove the burgers to a resting plate and let the burgers rest for a few minutes before dressing and serving.
5. While the burgers are resting, toast the pita breads in the air fryer for 2 minutes. Tuck the burgers into the toasted pita breads, or wrap the pitas around the burgers and serve with a tzatziki sauce or some mayonnaise.

Crispy Ham And Eggs

Servings: 3

Cooking Time: 9 Minutes

Ingredients:

- 2 cups Rice-puff cereal, such as Rice Krispies
- ¼ cup Maple syrup
- ½ pound ¼- to ½-inch-thick ham steak (gluten-free, if a concern)
- 1 tablespoon Unsalted butter
- 3 Large eggs
- ⅛ teaspoon Table salt
- ⅛ teaspoon Ground black pepper

Directions:

1. Preheat the air fryer to 400°F.
2. Pour the cereal into a food processor, cover, and process until finely ground. Pour the ground cereal into a shallow soup plate or a small pie plate.
3. Smear the maple syrup on both sides of the ham, then set the ham into the ground cereal. Turn a few times, pressing gently, until evenly coated.
4. Set the ham steak in the basket and air-fry undisturbed for 5 minutes, or until browned.
5. Meanwhile, melt the butter in a medium or large nonstick skillet set over medium heat. Crack the eggs into the skillet and cook until the whites are set and the yolks are hot, about 3 minutes (or 4 minutes for a more set yolk.) Season with the salt and pepper.
6. When the ham is ready, transfer it to a serving platter, then slip the eggs from the skillet on top of it. Divide into portions to serve.

Peachy Pork Chops

Servings: 2

Cooking Time: 20 Minutes

Ingredients:

- 2 tbsp peach preserves
- 2 tbsp tomato paste
- 1 tbsp Dijon mustard
- 1 tsp BBQ sauce
- 1 tbsp lime juice
- 1 tbsp olive oil
- 2 cloves garlic, minced
- 2 pork chops

Directions:

1. Whisk all ingredients in a bowl until well mixed and let chill covered in the fridge for 30 minutes. Preheat air

fryer to 350ºF. Place pork chops in the frying basket and Air Fry for 12 minutes or until cooked through and tender. Transfer the chops to a cutting board and let sit for 5 minutes before serving.

Steak Fajitas

Servings: 4

Cooking Time: 20 Minutes

Ingredients:

- 1 lb beef flank steak, cut into strips
- 1 red bell pepper, cut into strips
- 1 green bell pepper, cut into strips
- ½ cup sweet corn
- 1 shallot, cut into strips
- 2 tbsp fajita seasoning
- Salt and pepper to taste
- 2 tbsp olive oil
- 8 flour tortillas

Directions:

1. Preheat air fryer to 380°F. Combine beef, bell peppers, corn, shallot, fajita seasoning, salt, pepper, and olive oil in a large bowl until well mixed.
2. Pour the beef and vegetable mixture into the air fryer. Air Fry for 9-11 minutes, shaking the basket once halfway through. Spoon a portion of the beef and vegetables in each of the tortillas and top with favorite toppings. Serve.

Fish And Seafood Recipes

Corn & Shrimp Boil

Servings: 4

Cooking Time: 40 Minutes

Ingredients:

- 8 frozen "mini" corn on the cob
- 1 tbsp smoked paprika
- 2 tsp dried thyme
- 1 tsp dried marjoram
- 1 tsp sea salt
- 1 tsp garlic powder
- 1 tsp onion powder
- 1 tsp cayenne pepper

- 1 lb baby potatoes, halved
- 1 tbsp olive oil
- 1 lb peeled shrimp, deveined
- 1 avocado, sliced

Directions:

1. Preheat the air fryer to 370°F. Combine the paprika, thyme, marjoram, salt, garlic, onion, and cayenne and mix well. Pour into a small glass jar. Add the potatoes, corn, and olive oil to the frying basket and sprinkle with 2 tsp of the spice mix and toss. Air Fry for 15 minutes, shaking the basket once until tender. Remove and set aside. Put the shrimp in the frying basket and sprinkle with 2 tsp of the spice mix. Air Fry for 5-8 minutes, shaking once until shrimp are tender and pink. Combine all the ingredients in the frying basket and sprinkle with 2 tsp of the spice mix. Toss to coat and cook for 1-2 more minutes or until hot. Serve topped with avocado.

Salmon Puttanesca En Papillotte With Zucchini

Servings: 2

Cooking Time: 17 Minutes

Ingredients:

- 1 small zucchini, sliced into ¼-inch thick half moons
- 1 teaspoon olive oil
- salt and freshly ground black pepper
- 2 (5-ounce) salmon fillets
- 1 beefsteak tomato, chopped (about 1 cup)
- 1 tablespoon capers, rinsed
- 10 black olives, pitted and sliced
- 2 tablespoons dry vermouth or white wine 2 tablespoons butter
- ¼ cup chopped fresh basil, chopped

Directions:

1. Preheat the air fryer to 400°F.
2. Toss the zucchini with the olive oil, salt and freshly ground black pepper. Transfer the zucchini into the air fryer basket and air-fry for 5 minutes, shaking the basket once or twice during the cooking process.
3. Cut out 2 large rectangles of parchment paper – about 13-inches by 15-inches each. Divide the air-fried zucchini between the two pieces of parchment paper, placing the vegetables in the center of each rectangle.
4. Place a fillet of salmon on each pile of zucchini. Season the fish very well with salt and pepper. Toss the tomato, capers, olives and vermouth (or white wine) together in a bowl. Divide the tomato mixture between the two fish packages, placing it on top of the fish fillets and pouring any juice out of the bowl onto the fish. Top each fillet with a tablespoon of butter.
5. Fold up each parchment square. Bring two edges together and fold them over a few times, leaving some space above the fish. Twist the open sides together and upwards so they can serve as handles for the packet, but don't let them extend beyond the top of the air fryer basket.
6. Place the two packages into the air fryer and air-fry at 400°F for 12 minutes. The packages should be puffed up and slightly browned when fully cooked. Once cooked, let the fish sit in the parchment for 2 minutes.
7. Serve the fish in the parchment paper, or if desired, remove the parchment paper before serving. Garnish with a little fresh basil.

Cheesy Salmon-stuffed Avocados

Servings: 2

Cooking Time: 20 Minutes

Ingredients:

- ¼ cup apple cider vinegar
- 1 tsp granular sugar
- ¼ cup sliced red onions
- 2 oz cream cheese, softened
- 1 tbsp capers
- 2 halved avocados, pitted
- 4 oz smoked salmon
- ¼ tsp dried dill
- 2 cherry tomatoes, halved
- 1 tbsp cilantro, chopped

Directions:

1. Warm apple vinegar and sugar in a saucepan over medium heat and simmer for 4 minutes until boiling. Add in onion and turn the heat off. Let sit until ready to use. Drain before using. In a small bowl, combine cream cheese and capers. Let chill in the fridge until ready to use.
2. Preheat air fryer to 350ºF. Place avocado halves, cut sides-up, in the frying basket, and Air Fry for 4 minutes. Transfer avocado halves to 2 plates. Top with cream cheese mixture, smoked salmon, dill, red onions, tomato halves and cilantro. Serve immediately.

Breaded Parmesan Perch

Servings: 5

Cooking Time: 15 Minutes

Ingredients:

- ¼ cup grated Parmesan
- ½ tsp salt
- ¼ tsp paprika
- 1 tbsp chopped dill
- 1 tsp dried thyme
- 2 tsp Dijon mustard
- 2 tbsp bread crumbs
- 4 ocean perch fillets
- 1 lemon, quartered
- 2 tbsp chopped cilantro

Directions:

1. Preheat air fryer to 400°F. Combine salt, paprika, pepper, dill, mustard, thyme, Parmesan, and bread crumbs in a wide bowl. Coat all sides of the fillets in the breading, then transfer to the greased frying basket. Air Fry for 8 minutes until outside is golden and the inside is cooked through. Garnish with lemon wedges and sprinkle with cilantro. Serve and enjoy!

Shrimp-jalapeño Poppers In Prosciutto

Servings: 4

Cooking Time: 30 Minutes

Ingredients:

- 1 lb shelled tail on shrimp, deveined, sliced down the spine
- 2 jalapeños, diced
- 2 tbsp grated cheddar
- 3 tbsp mascarpone cheese
- ¼ tsp garlic powder
- 1 tbsp mayonnaise
- ¼ tsp ground black pepper
- 20 prosciutto slices
- ¼ cup chopped parsley
- 1 lemon

Directions:

1. Preheat air fryer at 400ºF. Combine the mascarpone and cheddar cheeses, jalapeños, garlic, mayonnaise, and black pepper in a bowl. Press cheese mixture into shrimp. Wrap 1 piece of prosciutto around each shrimp to hold in the cheese mixture. Place wrapped shrimp in the frying basket and Air Fry for 8-10 minutes, flipping once. To serve, scatter with parsley and squeeze lemon.

Mom´s Tuna Melt Toastie

Servings: 4

Cooking Time: 30 Minutes

Ingredients:

- 4 white bread slices
- 2 oz canned tuna
- 2 tbsp mayonnaise
- ½ lemon, zested and juiced
- Salt and pepper to taste
- ½ red onion, finely sliced
- 1 red tomato, sliced
- 4 cheddar cheese slices
- 2 tbsp butter, melted

Directions:

1. Preheat air fryer to 360°F. Put the butter-greased bread slices in the frying basket. Toast for 6 minutes. Meanwhile, mix the tuna, lemon juice and zest, salt, pepper, and mayonnaise in a small bowl. When the time is over, slide the frying basket out, flip the bread slices, and spread the tuna mixture evenly all over them. Cover with tomato slices, red onion, and cheddar cheese. Toast for 10 minutes or until the cheese is melted and lightly bubbling. Serve and enjoy!

Fried Scallops

Servings: 3

Cooking Time: 6 Minutes

Ingredients:

- ½ cup All-purpose flour or tapioca flour
- 1 Large egg(s), well beaten

- 2 cups Corn flake crumbs (gluten-free, if a concern)
- Up to 2 teaspoons Cayenne
- 1 teaspoon Celery seeds
- 1 teaspoon Table salt
- 1 pound Sea scallops
- Vegetable oil spray

Directions:

1. Preheat the air fryer to 400°F.
2. Set up and fill three shallow soup plates or small pie plates on your counter: one for the flour; one for the beaten egg(s); and one for the corn flake crumbs, stirred with the cayenne, celery seeds, and salt until well combined.
3. One by one, dip a scallop in the flour, turning it every way to coat it thoroughly. Gently shake off any excess flour, then dip the scallop in the egg(s), turning it again to coat all sides. Let any excess egg slip back into the rest, then set the scallop in the corn flake mixture. Turn it several times, pressing gently to get an even coating on the scallop all around. Generously coat the scallop with vegetable oil spray, then set it aside on a cutting board. Coat the remaining scallops in the same way.
4. Set the scallops in the basket with as much air space between them as possible. They should not touch. Air-fry undisturbed for 6 minutes, or until lightly browned and firm.
5. Use kitchen tongs to gently transfer the scallops to a wire rack. Cool for only a minute or two before serving.

Sinaloa Fish Fajitas

Servings: 4

Cooking Time: 30 Minutes

Ingredients:

- 1 lemon, thinly sliced
- 16 oz red snapper filets
- 1 tbsp olive oil
- 1 tbsp cayenne pepper
- ½ tsp salt
- 2 cups shredded coleslaw
- 1 carrot, shredded
- 2 tbsp orange juice
- ½ cup salsa
- 4 flour tortillas
- ½ cup sour cream
- 2 avocados, sliced

Directions:

1. Preheat the air fryer to 350°F. Lay the lemon slices at the bottom of the basket. Drizzle the fillets with olive oil and sprinkle with cayenne pepper and salt. Lay the fillets on top of the lemons and Bake for 6-9 minutes or until the fish easily flakes. While the fish cooks, toss the coleslaw, carrot, orange juice, and salsa in a bowl. When the fish is done, remove it and cover. Toss the lemons. Air Fry the tortillas for 2-3 minutes to warm up. Add the fish to the tortillas and top with a cabbage mix, sour cream, and avocados. Serve and enjoy!

Dilly Red Snapper

Servings: 4

Cooking Time: 40 Minutes

Ingredients:

- Salt and pepper to taste
- ½ tsp ground cumin
- ¼ tsp cayenne
- ¼ teaspoon paprika
- 1 whole red snapper
- 2 tbsp butter
- 2 garlic cloves, minced
- ¼ cup dill
- 4 lemon wedges

Directions:

1. Preheat air fryer to 360°F. Combine salt, pepper, cumin, paprika and cayenne in a bowl. Brush the fish with butter, then rub with the seasoning mix. Stuff the minced garlic and dill inside the cavity of the fish. Put the snapper into the basket of the air fryer and Roast for 20 minutes. Flip the snapper over and Roast for 15 more minutes. Serve with lemon wedges and enjoy!

Piña Colada Shrimp

Servings: 4

Cooking Time: 25 Minutes

Ingredients:

- 1 lb large shrimp, deveined and shelled
- 1 can crushed pineapple
- ½ cup sour cream
- ¼ cup pineapple preserves
- 2 egg whites
- 1 tbsp dark rum
- 2/3 cup cornstarch
- 2/3 cup sweetened coconut
- 1 cup panko bread crumbs

Directions:

1. Preheat air fryer to 400°F. Drain the crushed pineapple and reserve the juice. Next, transfer the pineapple to a small bowl and mix with sour cream and preserves. Set aside. In a shallow bowl, beat egg whites with 1 tbsp of the reserved pineapple juice and rum. On a separate plate, add the cornstarch. On another plate, stir together coconut and bread crumbs. Coat the shrimp with the cornstarch. Then, dip the shrimp into the egg white mixture. Shake off drips and then coat with the coconut mixture. Place the shrimp in the greased frying basket. Air Fry until crispy and golden, 7 minutes. Serve warm.

Lime Halibut Parcels

Servings: 4

Cooking Time: 45 Minutes

Ingredients:

- 1 lime, sliced
- 4 halibut fillets
- 1 tsp dried thyme
- Salt and pepper to taste
- 1 shredded carrot
- 1 red bell pepper, sliced
- ½ cup sliced celery
- 2 tbsp butter

Directions:

1. Preheat the air fryer to 400°F. Tear off four 14-inch lengths of parchment paper and fold each piece in half crosswise. Put the lime slices in the center of half of each piece of paper, then top with halibut. Sprinkle each filet with thyme, salt, and pepper, then top each with ¼ of the carrots, bell pepper, and celery. Add a dab of butter. Fold the parchment paper in half and crimp the edges all around to enclose the halibut and vegetables. Put one parchment bundle in the basket, add a raised rack, and add another bundle. Bake for 12-14 minutes or until the bundle puff up. The fish should flake with a fork; put the bundles in the oven to keep warm. Repeat for the second batch of parchment bundles. Hot steam will be released when the bundles are opened.

Fish Tacos With Hot Coleslaw

Servings: 4

Cooking Time: 25 Minutes

Ingredients:

- 2 cups shredded green cabbage
- ½ red onion, thinly sliced
- 1 jalapeño, thinly sliced
- 1 tsp lemon juice
- 1 tbsp chives, chopped
- 3 tbsp mayonnaise
- 1 tbsp hot sauce
- 2 tbsp chopped cilantro
- 1 tbsp apple cider vinegar
- Salt to taste
- 1 large egg, beaten
- 1 cup crushed tortilla chips
- 1 lb cod fillets, cubed
- 8 corn tortillas

Directions:

1. Mix the lemon juice, chives, mayonnaise, and hot sauce in a bowl until blended. Add the cabbage to a large bowl. Then add onion, jalapeño, cilantro, vinegar and salt. Toss until well mixed. Put in the fridge until ready to serve.
2. Preheat air fryer to 360°F. In one shallow bowl, add the beaten egg. In another shallow bowl, add the crushed tortilla chips. Salt the cod, then dip into the egg mixture. Allow excess to drip off. Next, dip into the crumbs, gently pressing into the crumbs. Place the fish in the greased frying basket and Air Fry for 6 minutes, flipping once until crispy and completely cooked. Place 2 warm tortillas on each plate. Top with cod cubes, ¼ cup of slaw, and drizzle with spicy mayo. Serve and enjoy!

Seared Scallops In Beurre Blanc

Servings: 4

Cooking Time: 15 Minutes

Ingredients:

- 1 lb sea scallops
- Salt and pepper to taste
- 2 tbsp butter, melted
- 1 lemon, zested and juiced
- 2 tbsp dry white wine

Directions:

1. Preheat the air fryer to 400°F. Sprinkle the scallops with salt and pepper, then set in a bowl. Combine the butter, lemon zest, lemon juice, and white wine in another bowl; mix well. Put the scallops in a baking pan and drizzle over them the mixture. Air Fry for 8-11 minutes, flipping over at about 5 minutes until opaque. Serve and enjoy!

Easy Asian-style Tuna

Servings: 4

Cooking Time: 25 Minutes

Ingredients:

- 1 jalapeño pepper, minced
- ½ tsp Chinese five-spice
- 4 tuna steaks
- ½ tsp toasted sesame oil
- 2 garlic cloves, grated
- 1 tbsp grated fresh ginger
- Black pepper to taste
- 2 tbsp lemon juice

Directions:

1. Preheat air fryer to 380°F. Pour sesame oil over the tuna steaks and let them sit while you make the marinade. Combine the jalapeño, garlic, ginger, five-spice powder, black pepper, and lemon juice in a bowl, then brush the mix on the fish. Let it sit for 10 minutes. Air Fry the tuna in the fryer for 6-11 minutes until it is cooked through and flakes easily when pressed with a fork. Serve warm.

Hot Calamari Rings

Servings: 4

Cooking Time: 25 Minutes

Ingredients:

- ½ cup all-purpose flour
- 2 tsp hot chili powder
- 2 eggs
- 1 tbsp milk

- 1 cup bread crumbs
- Salt and pepper to taste
- 1 lb calamari rings
- 1 lime, quartered
- ½ cup aioli sauce

Directions:

1. Preheat air fryer at 400ºF. In a shallow bowl, add flour and hot chili powder. In another bowl, mix the eggs and milk. In a third bowl, mix the breadcrumbs, salt and pepper. Dip calamari rings in flour mix first, then in eggs mix and shake off excess. Then, roll ring through breadcrumb mixture. Place calamari rings in the greased frying basket and Air Fry for 4 minutes, tossing once. Squeeze lime quarters over calamari. Serve with aioli sauce.

Horseradish Tuna Croquettes

Servings: 4

Cooking Time: 40 Minutes

Ingredients:

- 1 can tuna in water, drained
- 1/3 cup mayonnaise
- 1 tbsp minced celery
- 1 green onion, sliced
- 2 tsp dried dill
- 1 tsp lime juice
- 1 cup bread crumbs
- 1 egg
- 1 tsp prepared horseradish

Directions:

1. Preheat air fryer to 370ºF. Add the tuna, mayonnaise, celery, green onion, dill, lime juice, ¼ cup bread crumbs, egg, and horseradish in a bowl and mix to combine. Mold the mixture into 12 rectangular mound shapes. Roll each croquette in a shallow dish with 3/4 cup of bread crumbs. Place croquettes in the lightly greased frying basket and Air Fry for 12 minutes on all sides. Serve.

Tilapia Al Pesto

Servings: 4

Cooking Time: 25 Minutes

Ingredients:

- 4 tilapia fillets
- 1 egg
- 2 tbsp buttermilk
- 1 cup crushed cornflakes
- Salt and pepper to taste
- 4 tsp pesto
- 2 tbsp butter, melted
- 4 lemon wedges

Directions:

1. Preheat air fryer to 350°F. Whisk egg and buttermilk in a bowl. In another bowl, combine cornflakes, salt, and pepper. Spread 1 tsp of pesto on each tilapia fillet, then tightly roll the fillet from one short end to the other. Secure with a toothpick. Dip each fillet in the egg mixture and dredge in the cornflake mixture. Place fillets in the greased frying basket, drizzle with melted butter, and Air Fry for 6 minutes. Let rest onto a serving dish for 5 minutes before removing the toothpicks. Serve with lemon wedges.

Holiday Shrimp Scampi

Servings: 4

Cooking Time: 25 Minutes

Ingredients:

- 1 ½ lb peeled shrimp, deveined
- ¼ tsp lemon pepper seasoning
- 6 garlic cloves, minced
- 1 tsp salt
- ½ tsp grated lemon zest
- 3 tbsp fresh lemon juice
- 3 tbsp sunflower oil
- 3 tbsp butter
- 2 tsp fresh thyme leaves
- 1 lemon, cut into wedges

Directions:

1. Preheat the air fryer to 400°F. Combine the shrimp and garlic in a cake pan, then sprinkle with salt and lemon pepper seasoning. Toss to coat, then add the lemon zest, lemon juice, oil, and butter. Place the cake pan in the frying basket and Bake for 10-13 minutes, stirring once until no longer pink. Sprinkle with thyme leaves. Serve hot with lemon wedges on the side.

Fish And "chips"

Servings: 2

Cooking Time: 10 Minutes

Ingredients:

- ½ cup flour
- ½ teaspoon paprika
- ¼ teaspoon ground white pepper (or freshly ground black pepper)
- 1 egg
- ¼ cup mayonnaise
- 2 cups salt & vinegar kettle cooked potato chips, coarsely crushed
- 12 ounces cod
- tartar sauce
- lemon wedges

Directions:

1. Set up a dredging station. Combine the flour, paprika and pepper in a shallow dish. Combine the egg and mayonnaise in a second shallow dish. Place the crushed potato chips in a third shallow dish.
2. Cut the cod into 6 pieces. Dredge each piece of fish in the flour, then dip it into the egg mixture and then place it into the crushed potato chips. Make sure all sides of the fish are covered and pat the chips gently onto the

fish so they stick well.
3. Preheat the air fryer to 370°F.
4. Place the coated fish fillets into the air fry basket. (It is ok if a couple of pieces slightly overlap or rest on top of other fillets in order to fit everything in the basket.)
5. Air-fry for 10 minutes, gently turning the fish over halfway through the cooking time.
6. Transfer the fish to a platter and serve with tartar sauce and lemon wedges.

Lemon-dill Salmon Burgers

Servings: 4

Cooking Time: 8 Minutes

Ingredients:

- 2 (6-ounce) fillets of salmon, finely chopped by hand or in a food processor
- 1 cup fine breadcrumbs
- 1 teaspoon freshly grated lemon zest
- 2 tablespoons chopped fresh dill weed
- 1 teaspoon salt
- freshly ground black pepper
- 2 eggs, lightly beaten
- 4 brioche or hamburger buns
- lettuce, tomato, red onion, avocado, mayonnaise or mustard, to serve

Directions:

1. Preheat the air fryer to 400°F.
2. Combine all the ingredients in a bowl. Mix together well and divide into four balls. Flatten the balls into patties, making an indentation in the center of each patty with your thumb (this will help the burger stay flat as it cooks) and flattening the sides of the burgers so that they fit nicely into the air fryer basket.
3. Transfer the burgers to the air fryer basket and air-fry for 4 minutes. Flip the burgers over and air-fry for another 3 to 4 minutes, until nicely browned and firm to the touch.
4. Serve on soft brioche buns with your choice of topping – lettuce, tomato, red onion, avocado, mayonnaise or mustard.

Vegetarians Recipes

Party Giant Nachos

Servings: 2

Cooking Time: 20 Minutes

Ingredients:

- 2 tbsp sour cream

- ½ tsp chili powder
- Salt to taste
- 2 soft corn tortillas
- 2 tsp avocado oil
- ½ cup refried beans
- ¼ cup cheddar cheese shreds
- 2 tbsp Parmesan cheese
- 2 tbsp sliced black olives
- ¼ cup torn iceberg lettuce
- ¼ cup baby spinach
- ½ sliced avocado
- 1 tomato, diced
- 2 lime wedges

Directions:

1. Preheat air fryer at 400ºF. Whisk the sour cream, chili powder, and salt in a small bowl. Brush tortillas with avocado oil and season one side with salt. Place tortillas in the frying basket and Bake for 3 minutes. Set aside.
2. Layer the refried beans, Parmesan and cheddar cheeses in the tortillas. Place them back into the basket and Bake for 2 minutes. Divide tortillas into 2 serving plates. Top each tortilla with black olives, baby spinach, lettuce, and tomatoes. Dollop sour cream mixture on each. Serve with lime and avocado wedges on the side.

Vietnamese Gingered Tofu

Servings: 4

Cooking Time: 25 Minutes

Ingredients:

- 1 package extra-firm tofu, cubed
- 4 tsp shoyu
- 1 tsp onion powder
- ½ tsp garlic powder
- ½ tsp ginger powder
- ½ tsp turmeric powder
- Black pepper to taste
- 2 tbsp nutritional yeast
- 1 tsp dried rosemary
- 1 tsp dried dill
- 2 tsp cornstarch
- 2 tsp sunflower oil

Directions:

1. Sprinkle the tofu with shoyu and toss to coat. Add the onion, garlic, ginger, turmeric, and pepper. Gently toss to coat. Add the yeast, rosemary, dill, and cornstarch. Toss to coat. Dribble with the oil and toss again.
2. Preheat air fryer to 390°F. Spray the fryer basket with oil, put the tofu in the basket and Bake for 7 minutes. Remove, shake gently, and cook for another 7 minutes or until the tofu is crispy and golden. Serve warm.

Falafels

Servings: 12

Cooking Time: 10 Minutes

Ingredients:

- 1 pouch falafel mix
- 2-3 tablespoons plain breadcrumbs
- oil for misting or cooking spray

Directions:

1. Prepare falafel mix according to package directions.
2. Preheat air fryer to 390°F.
3. Place breadcrumbs in shallow dish or on wax paper.
4. Shape falafel mixture into 12 balls and flatten slightly. Roll in breadcrumbs to coat all sides and mist with oil or cooking spray.
5. Place falafels in air fryer basket in single layer and cook for 5 minutes. Shake basket, and continue cooking for 5 minutes, until they brown and are crispy.

Sushi-style Deviled Eggs

Servings: 4

Cooking Time: 20 Minutes

Ingredients:

- ¼ cup crabmeat, shells discarded
- 4 eggs
- 2 tbsp mayonnaise
- ½ tsp soy sauce
- ¼ avocado, diced
- ¼ tsp wasabi powder
- 2 tbsp diced cucumber
- 1 sheet nori, sliced
- 8 jarred pickled ginger slices
- 1 tsp toasted sesame seeds
- 2 spring onions, sliced

Directions:

1. Preheat air fryer to 260°F. Place the eggs in muffin cups to avoid bumping around and cracking during the cooking process. Add silicone cups to the frying basket and Air Fry for 15 minutes. Remove and plunge the eggs immediately into an ice bath to cool, about 5 minutes. Carefully peel and slice them in half lengthwise. Spoon yolks into a separate medium bowl and arrange white halves on a large plate. Mash the yolks with a fork. Stir in mayonnaise, soy sauce, avocado, and wasabi powder until smooth. Mix in cucumber and spoon into white halves. Scatter eggs with crabmeat, nori, pickled ginger, spring onions and sesame seeds to serve.

Vegetarian Shepherd's Pie

Servings: 4

Cooking Time: 40 Minutes

Ingredients:

- 1 russet potato, peeled and diced

- 1 tbsp olive oil
- 2 tbsp balsamic vinegar
- ¼ cup cheddar shreds
- 2 tbsp milk
- Salt and pepper to taste
- 2 tsp avocado oil
- 1 cup beefless grounds
- ½ onion, diced
- 3 cloves garlic
- 1 carrot, diced
- ¼ diced green bell peppers
- 1 celery stalk, diced
- 2/3 cup tomato sauce
- 1 tsp chopped rosemary
- 1 tbsp sesame seeds
- 1 tsp thyme leaves
- 1 lemon

Directions:

1. Add salted water to a pot over high heat and bring it to a boil. Add in diced potatoes and cook for 5 minutes until fork tender. Drain and transfer it to a bowl. Add in the olive oil cheddar shreds, milk, salt, and pepper and mash it until smooth. Set the potato topping aside.
2. Preheat air fryer at 350ºF. Place avocado oil, beefless grounds, garlic, onion, carrot, bell pepper, and celery in a skillet over medium heat and cook for 4 minutes until the veggies are tender. Stir in the remaining ingredients and turn the heat off. Spoon the filling into a greased cake pan. Top with the potato topping.
3. Using tines of a fork, create shallow lines along the top of mashed potatoes. Place cake pan in the frying basket and Bake for 12 minutes. Let rest for 10 minutes before serving sprinkled with sesame seeds and squeezed lemon.

Spinach & Brie Frittata

Servings: 4

Cooking Time: 25 Minutes

Ingredients:

- 5 eggs
- Salt and pepper to taste
- ½ cup baby spinach
- 1 shallot, diced
- 4 oz brie cheese, cubed
- 1 tomato, sliced

Directions:

1. Preheat air fryer to 320ºF. Whisk all ingredients, except for the tomato slices, in a bowl. Transfer to a baking pan greased with olive oil and top with tomato slices. Place the pan in the frying basket and Bake for 14 minutes. Let cool for 5 minutes before slicing. Serve and enjoy!

Cheese Ravioli

Servings: 4

Cooking Time: 9 Minutes

Ingredients:

- 1 egg
- ¼ cup milk
- 1 cup breadcrumbs
- 2 teaspoons Italian seasoning
- ⅛ teaspoon ground rosemary
- ¼ teaspoon basil
- ¼ teaspoon parsley
- 9-ounce package uncooked cheese ravioli
- ¼ cup flour
- oil for misting or cooking spray

Directions:

1. Preheat air fryer to 390°F.
2. In a medium bowl, beat together egg and milk.
3. In a large plastic bag, mix together the breadcrumbs, Italian seasoning, rosemary, basil, and parsley.
4. Place all the ravioli and the flour in a bag or a bowl with a lid and shake to coat.
5. Working with a handful at a time, drop floured ravioli into egg wash. Remove ravioli, letting excess drip off and place in bag with breadcrumbs.
6. When all ravioli are in the breadcrumbs' bag, shake well to coat all pieces.
7. Dump enough ravioli into air fryer basket to form one layer. Mist with oil or cooking spray. Dump the remaining ravioli on top of the first layer and mist with oil.
8. Cook for 5 minutes. Shake well and spray with oil. Break apart any ravioli stuck together and spray any spots you missed the first time.
9. Cook 4 minutes longer, until ravioli puff up and are crispy golden brown.

Crunchy Rice Paper Samosas

Servings: 2

Cooking Time: 20 Minutes

Ingredients:

- 1 boiled potato, mashed
- ¼ cup green peas
- 1 tsp garam masala powder
- ½ tsp ginger garlic paste
- ½ tsp cayenne pepper
- ½ tsp turmeric powder
- Salt and pepper to taste
- 3 rice paper wrappers

Directions:

1. Preheat air fryer to 350°F. Place the mashed potatoes in a bowl. Add the peas, garam masala powder, ginger garlic paste, cayenne pepper, turmeric powder, salt, and pepper and stir until ingredients are evenly blended.
2. Lay the rice paper wrappers out on a lightly floured surface. Divide the potato mixture between the wrappers and fold the top edges over to seal. Transfer the samosas to the greased frying basket and Air Fry for 15 minutes, flipping once until the samosas are crispy and flaky. Remove and leave to cool for 5 minutes. Serve and enjoy!

Roasted Veggie Bowls

Servings: 4

Cooking Time: 30 Minutes

Ingredients:

- 1 cup Brussels sprouts, trimmed and quartered
- ½ onion, cut into half-moons
- ½ cup green beans, chopped
- 1 cup broccoli florets
- 1 red bell pepper, sliced
- 1 yellow bell pepper, sliced
- 1 tbsp olive oil
- ½ tsp chili powder
- ¼ tsp ground cumin
- ¼ tsp ground coriander

Directions:

1. Preheat air fryer to 350ºF. Combine all ingredients in a bowl. Place veggie mixture in the frying basket and Air Fry for 15 minutes, tossing every 5 minutes. Divide between 4 medium bowls and serve.

Veggie Samosas

Servings: 6

Cooking Time: 30 Minutes

Ingredients:

- 2 tbsp cream cheese, softened
- 3 tbsp minced onion
- 2 garlic cloves, minced
- 2 tbsp grated carrots
- 3 tsp olive oil
- 3 tbsp cooked green lentils
- 6 phyllo dough sheets

Directions:

1. Preheat air fryer to 390ºF. Toss the onion, garlic, carrots, and some oil in a baking pan and stir. Place in the fryer and Air Fry for 2-4 minutes until the veggies are soft. Pour into a bowl. Add the lentils and cream cheese; let chill.
2. To make the dough, first lay a sheet of phyllo on a clean workspace and spritz with some olive oil, then add a second sheet on top. Repeat with the rest of the phyllo sheets until you have 3 stacks of 2 layers. Cut the stacks into 4 lengthwise strips. Add 2 tsp of the veggie mix at the bottom of each strip, then make a triangle by lifting one corner over the filling. Continue the triangle making, like folding a flag, and seal with water. Repeat until all strips are filled and folded. Bake the samosas in the air fryer for 4-7 minutes, until golden and crisp. Serve warm.

Cheesy Veggie Frittata

Servings: 2

Cooking Time: 65 Minutes

Ingredients:

- 4 oz Bella mushrooms, chopped
- ¼ cup halved grape tomatoes
- 1 cup baby spinach
- 1/3 cup chopped leeks
- 1 baby carrot, chopped
- 4 eggs
- ½ cup grated cheddar
- 1 tbsp milk
- ¼ tsp garlic powder
- ¼ tsp dried oregano
- Salt and pepper to taste

Directions:

1. Preheat air fryer to 300°F. Crack the eggs into a bowl and beat them with a fork or whisk. Mix in the remaining ingredients until well combined. Pour into a greased cake pan. Put the pan into the frying basket and Bake for 20-23 minutes or until eggs are set in the center. Remove from the fryer. Cut into halves and serve.

General Tso's Cauliflower

Servings: 4

Cooking Time: 15 Minutes

Ingredients:

- 1 head cauliflower cut into florets
- ¾ cup all-purpose flour, divided*
- 3 eggs, lightly beaten
- 1 cup panko breadcrumbs*
- canola or peanut oil, in a spray bottle
- 2 tablespoons oyster sauce
- ¼ cup soy sauce
- 2 teaspoons chili paste
- 2 tablespoons rice wine vinegar
- 2 tablespoons sugar
- ¼ cup water
- white or brown rice for serving
- steamed broccoli

Directions:

1. Set up dredging station using three bowls. Place the cauliflower in a large bowl and sprinkle ¼ cup of the flour over the top. Place the eggs in a second bowl and combine the panko breadcrumbs and remaining ½ cup flour in a third bowl. Toss the cauliflower in the flour to coat all the florets thoroughly. Dip the cauliflower florets in the eggs and finally toss them in the breadcrumbs to coat on all sides. Place the coated cauliflower florets on a baking sheet and spray generously with canola or peanut oil.
2. Preheat the air fryer to 400°F.
3. Air-fry the cauliflower at 400°F for 15 minutes, flipping the florets over for the last 3 minutes of the cooking process and spraying again with oil.
4. While the cauliflower is air-frying, make the General Tso Sauce. Combine the oyster sauce, soy sauce, chili paste, rice wine vinegar, sugar and water in a saucepan and bring the mixture to a boil on the stove top. Low

er the heat and let it simmer for 10 minutes, stirring occasionally.
5. When the timer is up on the air fryer, transfer the cauliflower to a large bowl, pour the sauce over it all and toss to coat. Serve with white or brown rice and some steamed broccoli.

Harissa Veggie Fries

Servings: 4

Cooking Time: 55 Minutes

Ingredients:

- 1 pound red potatoes, cut into rounds
- 1 onion, diced
- 1 green bell pepper, diced
- 1 red bell pepper, diced
- 2 tbsp olive oil
- Salt and pepper to taste
- ¾ tsp garlic powder
- ¾ tsp harissa seasoning

Directions:

1. Combine all ingredients in a large bowl and mix until potatoes are well coated and seasoned. Preheat air fryer to 350°F. Pour all of the contents in the bowl into the frying basket. Bake for 35 minutes, shaking every 10 minutes, until golden brown and soft. Serve hot.

Pineapple & Veggie Souvlaki

Servings: 4

Cooking Time: 35 Minutes

Ingredients:

- 1 can pineapple rings in pineapple juice
- 1 red bell pepper, stemmed and seeded
- 1/3 cup butter
- 2 tbsp apple cider vinegar
- 2 tbsp hot sauce
- 1 tbsp allspice
- 1 tsp ground nutmeg
- 16 oz feta cheese
- 1 red onion, peeled
- 8 mushrooms, quartered

Directions:

1. Preheat air fryer to 400°F. Whisk the butter, pineapple juice, apple vinegar, hot sauce, allspice, and nutmeg until smooth. Set aside. Slice feta cheese into 16 cubes, then the bell pepper into 16 chunks, and finally red onion into 8 wedges, separating each wedge into 2 pieces.
2. Cut pineapple ring into quarters. Place veggie cubes and feta into the butter bowl and toss to coat. Thread the veggies, tofu, and pineapple onto 8 skewers, alternating 16 pieces on each skewer. Grill for 15 minutes until golden brown and cooked. Serve warm.

Arancini With Marinara

Servings: 6

Cooking Time: 15 Minutes

Ingredients:

- 2 cups cooked rice
- 1 cup grated Parmesan cheese
- 1 egg, whisked
- ¼ teaspoon dried thyme
- ½ teaspoon dried oregano
- ½ teaspoon dried basil
- ½ teaspoon dried parsley
- 1 teaspoon salt
- ¼ teaspoon paprika
- 1 cup breadcrumbs
- 4 ounces mozzarella, cut into 24 cubes
- 2 cups marinara sauce

Directions:

1. In a large bowl, mix together the rice, Parmesan cheese, and egg.
2. In another bowl, mix together the thyme, oregano, basil, parsley, salt, paprika, and breadcrumbs.
3. Form 24 rice balls with the rice mixture. Use your thumb to make an indentation in the center and stuff 1 cube of mozzarella in the center of the rice; close the ball around the cheese.
4. Roll the rice balls in the seasoned breadcrumbs until all are coated.
5. Preheat the air fryer to 400°F.
6. Place the rice balls in the air fryer basket and coat with cooking spray. Cook for 8 minutes, shake the basket and cook another 7 minutes.
7. Heat the marinara sauce in a saucepan until warm. Serve sauce as a dip for arancini.

Tropical Salsa

Servings: 4

Cooking Time: 15 Minutes

Ingredients:

- 1 cup pineapple cubes
- ½ apple, cubed
- Salt to taste
- ¼ tsp olive oil
- 2 tomatoes, diced
- 1 avocado, diced
- 3-4 strawberries, diced
- ¼ cup diced red onion
- 1 tbsp chopped cilantro
- 1 tbsp chopped parsley
- 2 cloves garlic, minced
- ½ tsp granulated sugar
- ½ lime, juiced

Directions:

1. Preheat air fryer at 400ºF. Combine pineapple cubes, apples, olive oil, and salt in a bowl. Place pineapple in the greased frying basket, and Air Fry for 8 minutes, shaking once. Transfer it to a bowl. Toss in tomatoes, avocado, strawberries, onion, cilantro, parsley, garlic, sugar, lime juice, and salt. Let chill in the fridge before using.

Corn And Pepper Jack Chile Rellenos With Roasted Tomato Sauce

Servings: 3

Cooking Time: 30 Minutes

Ingredients:

- 3 Poblano peppers
- 1 cup all-purpose flour*
- salt and freshly ground black pepper
- 2 eggs, lightly beaten
- 1 cup plain breadcrumbs*
- olive oil, in a spray bottle
- Sauce
- 2 cups cherry tomatoes
- 1 Jalapeño pepper, halved and seeded
- 1 clove garlic
- ¼ red onion, broken into large pieces
- 1 tablespoon olive oil
- salt, to taste
- 2 tablespoons chopped fresh cilantro
- Filling
- olive oil
- ¼ red onion, finely chopped
- 1 teaspoon minced garlic
- 1 cup corn kernels, fresh or frozen
- 2 cups grated pepper jack cheese

Directions:

1. Start by roasting the peppers. Preheat the air fryer to 400°F. Place the peppers into the air fryer basket and air-fry at 400°F for 10 minutes, turning them over halfway through the cooking time. Remove the peppers from the basket and cover loosely with foil.
2. While the peppers are cooling, make the roasted tomato sauce. Place all sauce Ingredients except for the cilantro into the air fryer basket and air-fry at 400°F for 10 minutes, shaking the basket once or twice. When the sauce Ingredients have finished air-frying, transfer everything to a blender or food processor and blend or process to a smooth sauce, adding a little warm water to get the desired consistency. Season to taste with salt, add the cilantro and set aside.
3. While the sauce Ingredients are cooking in the air fryer, make the filling. Heat a skillet on the stovetop over medium heat. Add the olive oil and sauté the red onion and garlic for 4 to 5 minutes. Transfer the onion and garlic to a bowl, stir in the corn and cheese, and set aside.
4. Set up a dredging station with three shallow dishes. Place the flour, seasoned with salt and pepper, in the first shallow dish. Place the eggs in the second dish, and fill the third shallow dish with the breadcrumbs. When the peppers have cooled, carefully slice into one side of the pepper to create an opening. Pull the seeds out of the peppers and peel away the skins, trying not to tear the pepper. Fill each pepper with some of the corn and cheese filling and close the pepper up again by folding one side of the opening over the other. Carefully roll

each pepper in the seasoned flour, then into the egg and finally into the breadcrumbs to coat on all sides, trying not to let the pepper fall open. Spray the peppers on all sides with a little olive oil.
5. Air-fry two peppers at a time at 350°F for 6 minutes. Turn the peppers over and air-fry for another 4 minutes. Serve the peppers warm on a bed of the roasted tomato sauce.

Cheesy Eggplant Lasagna

Servings: 4

Cooking Time: 40 Minutes

Ingredients:

- ¾ cup chickpea flour
- ½ cup milk
- 3 tbsp lemon juice
- 1 tbsp chili sauce
- 2 tsp allspice
- 2 cups panko bread crumbs
- 1 eggplant, sliced
- 2 cups jarred tomato sauce
- ½ cup ricotta cheese
- 1/3 cup mozzarella cheese

Directions:

1. Preheat air fryer to 400°F. Whisk chickpea flour, milk, lemon juice, chili sauce, and allspice until smooth. Set aside. On a plate, put the breadcrumbs. Submerge each eggplant slice into the batter, shaking off any excess and dip into the breadcrumbs until well coated. Bake for 10 minutes, turning once. Let cool slightly.
2. Spread 2 tbsp of tomato sauce at the bottom of a baking pan. Lay a single layer of eggplant slices, scatter with ricotta cheese and top with tomato sauce. Repeat the process until no ingredients are left. Scatter with mozzarella cheese on top and Bake at 350ºF for 10 minutes until the eggplants are cooked and the cheese golden brown. Serve immediately.

Egg Rolls

Servings: 4

Cooking Time: 8 Minutes

Ingredients:

- 1 clove garlic, minced
- 1 teaspoon sesame oil
- 1 teaspoon olive oil
- ½ cup chopped celery
- ½ cup grated carrots
- 2 green onions, chopped
- 2 ounces mushrooms, chopped
- 2 cups shredded Napa cabbage
- 1 teaspoon low-sodium soy sauce
- 1 teaspoon cornstarch
- salt
- 1 egg

- 1 tablespoon water
- 4 egg roll wraps
- olive oil for misting or cooking spray

Directions:

1. In a large skillet, sauté garlic in sesame and olive oils over medium heat for 1 minute.
2. Add celery, carrots, onions, and mushrooms to skillet. Cook 1 minute, stirring.
3. Stir in cabbage, cover, and cook for 1 minute or just until cabbage slightly wilts.
4. In a small bowl, mix soy sauce and cornstarch. Stir into vegetables to thicken. Remove from heat. Salt to taste if needed.
5. Beat together egg and water in a small bowl.
6. Divide filling into 4 portions and roll up in egg roll wraps. Brush all over with egg wash to seal.
7. Mist egg rolls very lightly with olive oil or cooking spray and place in air fryer basket.
8. Cook at 390°F for 4 minutes. Turn over and cook 4 more minutes, until golden brown and crispy.

Rigatoni With Roasted Onions, Fennel, Spinach And Lemon Pepper Ricotta

Servings: 2

Cooking Time: 13 Minutes

Ingredients:

- 1 red onion, rough chopped into large chunks
- 2 teaspoons olive oil, divided
- 1 bulb fennel, sliced ¼-inch thick
- ¾ cup ricotta cheese
- 1½ teaspoons finely chopped lemon zest, plus more for garnish
- 1 teaspoon lemon juice
- salt and freshly ground black pepper
- 8 ounces (½ pound) dried rigatoni pasta
- 3 cups baby spinach leaves

Directions:

1. Bring a large stockpot of salted water to a boil on the stovetop and Preheat the air fryer to 400°F.
2. While the water is coming to a boil, toss the chopped onion in 1 teaspoon of olive oil and transfer to the air fryer basket. Air-fry at 400°F for 5 minutes. Toss the sliced fennel with 1 teaspoon of olive oil and add this to the air fryer basket with the onions. Continue to air-fry at 400°F for 8 minutes, shaking the basket a few times during the cooking process.
3. Combine the ricotta cheese, lemon zest and juice, ¼ teaspoon of salt and freshly ground black pepper in a bowl and stir until smooth.
4. Add the dried rigatoni to the boiling water and cook according to the package directions. When the pasta is cooked al dente, reserve one cup of the pasta water and drain the pasta into a colander.
5. Place the spinach in a serving bowl and immediately transfer the hot pasta to the bowl, wilting the spinach. Add the roasted onions and fennel and toss together. Add a little pasta water to the dish if it needs moistening. Then, dollop the lemon pepper ricotta cheese on top and nestle it into the hot pasta. Garnish with more lemon zest if desired.

Vegetable Side Dishes Recipes

Garlicky Bell Pepper Mix

Servings: 4

Cooking Time: 30 Minutes

Ingredients:

- 2 tbsp vegetable oil
- ½ tsp dried cilantro
- 1 red bell pepper
- 1 yellow bell pepper
- 1 orange bell pepper
- 1 green bell pepper
- Salt and pepper to taste
- 1 head garlic

Directions:

1. Preheat air fryer to 330°F. Slice the peppers into 1-inch strips. Transfer them to a large bowl along with 1 tbsp of vegetable oil. Toss to coat. Season with cilantro, salt, and pepper. Cut the top of a garlic head and place it cut-side up on an oiled square of aluminium foil. Drizzle with vegetable oil and wrap completely in the foil.
2. Roast the wrapped garlic in the air fryer for 15 minutes. Next, add the pepper strips and roast until the peppers are tender and the garlic is soft, 6-8 minutes. Transfer the peppers to a serving dish. Remove the garlic and unwrap the foil carefully. Once cooled, squeeze the cloves out of the garlic head and mix into the peppers dish. Serve.

Thyme Sweet Potato Wedges

Servings: 4

Cooking Time: 30 Minutes

Ingredients:

- 2 peeled sweet potatoes, cubed
- ¼ cup grated Parmesan
- 1 tbsp olive oil
- Salt and pepper to taste
- ½ tsp dried thyme
- ½ tsp ground cumin

Directions:

1. Preheat air fryer to 330°F. Add sweet potato cubes to the frying basket, then drizzle with oil. Toss to gently coat. Season with salt, pepper, thyme, and cumin. Roast the potatoes for about 10 minutes. Shake the basket and continue roasting for another 10 minutes. Shake the basket again, this time adding Parmesan cheese. Shake and return to the air fryer. Roast until the potatoes are tender, 4-6 minutes. Serve and enjoy!

Teriyaki Tofu With Spicy Mayo

Servings: 2

Cooking Time: 35 Minutes + 1 Hour To Marinate

Ingredients:

- 1 scallion, chopped
- 7 oz extra-firm tofu, sliced
- 2 tbsp soy sauce
- 1 tsp toasted sesame oil
- 1 red chili, thinly sliced
- 1 tsp mirin
- 1 tsp light brown sugar
- 1 garlic clove, grated
- ½ tsp grated ginger
- 1/3 cup sesame seeds
- 1 egg
- 4 tsp mayonnaise
- 1 tbsp lime juice
- 1 tsp hot chili powder

Directions:

1. Squeeze most of the water from the tofu by lightly pressing the slices between two towels. Place the tofu in a baking dish. Use a whisk to mix soy sauce, sesame oil, red chili, mirin, brown sugar, garlic and ginger. Pour half of the marinade over the tofu. Using a spatula, carefully flip the tofu down and pour the other half of the marinade over. Refrigerate for 1 hour.
2. Preheat air fryer to 400°F. In a shallow plate, add sesame seeds. In another shallow plate, beat the egg. Remove the tofu from the refrigerator. Let any excess marinade drip off. Dip each piece in the egg mixture and then in the sesame seeds. Transfer to greased frying basket. Air Fry for 10 minutes, flipping once until toasted and crispy. Meanwhile, mix mayonnaise, lime juice, and hot chili powder and in a small bowl. Top with a dollop of hot chili mayo and some scallions. Serve and enjoy!

Spiced Pumpkin Wedges

Servings: 4

Cooking Time: 35 Minutes

Ingredients:

- 2 ½ cups pumpkin, cubed
- 2 tbsp olive oil
- Salt and pepper to taste
- ¼ tsp pumpkin pie spice
- 1 tbsp thyme
- ¼ cup grated Parmesan

Directions:

1. Preheat air fryer to 360°F. Put the cubed pumpkin with olive oil, salt, pumpkin pie spice, black pepper, and thyme in a bowl and stir until the pumpkin is well coated. Pour this mixture into the frying basket and Roast for 18-20 minutes, stirring once. Sprinkle the pumpkin with grated Parmesan. Serve and enjoy!

Sesame Carrots And Sugar Snap Peas

Cooking Time: 16 Minutes

Servings: 4

Ingredients:

- 1 pound carrots, peeled sliced on the bias (½-inch slices)
- 1 teaspoon olive oil
- salt and freshly ground black pepper
- ⅓ cup honey
- 1 tablespoon sesame oil
- 1 tablespoon soy sauce
- ½ teaspoon minced fresh ginger
- 4 ounces sugar snap peas (about 1 cup)
- 1½ teaspoons sesame seeds

Directions:

1. Preheat the air fryer to 360°F.
2. Toss the carrots with the olive oil, season with salt and pepper and air-fry for 10 minutes, shaking the basket once or twice during the cooking process.
3. Combine the honey, sesame oil, soy sauce and minced ginger in a large bowl. Add the sugar snap peas and the air-fried carrots to the honey mixture, toss to coat and return everything to the air fryer basket.
4. Turn up the temperature to 400°F and air-fry for an additional 6 minutes, shaking the basket once during the cooking process.
5. Transfer the carrots and sugar snap peas to a serving bowl. Pour the sauce from the bottom of the cooker over the vegetables and sprinkle sesame seeds over top. Serve immediately.

Asparagus

Servings: 4

Cooking Time: 9 Minutes

Ingredients:

- 1 bunch asparagus (approx. 1 pound), washed and trimmed
- ⅛ teaspoon dried tarragon, crushed
- salt and pepper
- 1 to 2 teaspoons extra-light olive oil

Directions:

1. Spread asparagus spears on cookie sheet or cutting board.
2. Sprinkle with tarragon, salt, and pepper.
3. Drizzle with 1 teaspoon of oil and roll the spears or mix by hand. If needed, add up to 1 more teaspoon of oil and mix again until all spears are lightly coated.
4. Place spears in air fryer basket. If necessary, bend the longer spears to make them fit. It doesn't matter if they don't lie flat.
5. Cook at 390°F for 5minutes. Shake basket or stir spears with a spoon.
6. Cook for an additional 4 minutes or just until crisp-tender.

Balsamic Green Beans With Bacon

Servings: 4

Cooking Time: 15 Minutes

Ingredients:

- 2 cups green beans, trimmed
- 1 tbsp butter, melted
- Salt and pepper to taste
- 1 bacon slice, diced
- 1 clove garlic, minced
- 1 tbsp balsamic vinegar

Directions:

1. Preheat air fryer to 375ºF. Combine green beans, butter, salt, and pepper in a bowl. Put the bean mixture in the frying basket and Air Fry for 5 minutes. Stir in bacon and Air Fry for 4 more minutes. Mix in garlic and cook for 1 minute. Transfer it to a serving dish, drizzle with balsamic vinegar and combine. Serve right away.

Buttery Radish Wedges

Servings: 2

Cooking Time: 20 Minutes

Ingredients:

- 2 tbsp butter, melted
- 2 cloves garlic, minced
- ¼ tsp salt
- 20 radishes, quartered
- 2 tbsp feta cheese crumbles
- 1 tbsp chopped parsley

Directions:

1. Preheat air fryer to 370ºF. Mix the butter, garlic, and salt in a bowl. Stir in radishes. Place the radish wedges in the frying basket and Roast for 10 minutes, shaking once. Transfer to a large serving dish and stir in feta cheese. Scatter with parsley and serve.

Fried Eggplant Balls

Servings: 4

Cooking Time: 40 Minutes

Ingredients:

- 1 medium eggplant (about 1 pound)
- olive oil
- salt and freshly ground black pepper
- 1 cup grated Parmesan cheese
- 2 cups fresh breadcrumbs
- 2 tablespoons chopped fresh parsley
- 2 tablespoons chopped fresh basil

- 1 clove garlic, minced
- 1 egg, lightly beaten
- ½ cup fine dried breadcrumbs

Directions:

1. Preheat the air fryer to 400°F.
2. Quarter the eggplant by cutting it in half both lengthwise and horizontally. Make a few slashes in the flesh of the eggplant but not through the skin. Brush the cut surface of the eggplant generously with olive oil and transfer to the air fryer basket, cut side up. Air-fry for 10 minutes. Turn the eggplant quarters cut side down and air-fry for another 15 minutes or until the eggplant is soft all the way through. You may need to rotate the pieces in the air fryer so that they cook evenly. Transfer the eggplant to a cutting board to cool.
3. Place the Parmesan cheese, the fresh breadcrumbs, fresh herbs, garlic and egg in a food processor. Scoop the flesh out of the eggplant, discarding the skin and any pieces that are tough. You should have about 1 to 1½ cups of eggplant. Add the eggplant to the food processor and process everything together until smooth. Season with salt and pepper. Refrigerate the mixture for at least 30 minutes.
4. Place the dried breadcrumbs into a shallow dish or onto a plate. Scoop heaping tablespoons of the eggplant mixture into the dried breadcrumbs. Roll the dollops of eggplant in the breadcrumbs and then shape into small balls. You should have 16 to 18 eggplant balls at the end. Refrigerate until you are ready to air-fry.
5. Preheat the air fryer to 350°F.
6. Spray the eggplant balls and the air fryer basket with olive oil. Air-fry the eggplant balls for 15 minutes, rotating the balls during the cooking process to brown evenly.

Patatas Bravas

Servings: 4

Cooking Time: 35 Minutes

Ingredients:

- 1 lb baby potatoes
- 1 onion, chopped
- 4 garlic cloves, minced
- 2 jalapeño peppers, minced
- 2 tsp olive oil
- 2 tsp Chile de Árbol, ground
- ½ tsp ground cumin
- ½ tsp dried oregano

Directions:

1. Preheat air fryer to 370°F. Put the baby potatoes, onion, garlic, and jalapeños in a bowl, stir, then pour in the olive oil and stir again to coat. Season with ground chile de Árbol, cumin, and oregano, and stir once again. Put the bowl in the air fryer and Air Fry for 22-28 minutes, shake the bowl once. Serve hot.

Rich Baked Sweet Potatoes

Servings: 2

Cooking Time: 55 Minutes

Ingredients:

- 1 lb sweet potatoes, scrubbed and perforated with a fork
- 2 tsp olive oil

- Salt and pepper to taste
- 2 tbsp butter
- 3 tbsp honey

Directions:

1. Preheat air fryer at 400ºF. Mix olive oil, salt, black pepper, and honey. Brush with the prepared mix over both sweet potatoes. Place them in the frying basket and Bake for 45 minutes, turning at 30 minutes mark. Let cool on a cutting board for 10 minutes until cool enough to handle. Slice each potato lengthwise. Press ends of one potato together to open up the slices. Top with butter to serve.

Green Dip With Pine Nuts

Servings: 3

Cooking Time: 30 Minutes

Ingredients:

- 10 oz canned artichokes, chopped
- 2 tsp grated Parmesan cheese
- 10 oz spinach, chopped
- 2 scallions, finely chopped
- ½ cup pine nuts
- ½ cup milk
- 3 tbsp lemon juice
- 2 tsp tapioca flour
- 1 tsp allspice

Directions:

1. Preheat air fryer to 360°F. Arrange spinach, artichokes, and scallions in a pan. Set aside. In a food processor, blitz the pine nuts, milk, lemon juice, Parmesan cheese, flour, and allspice on high until smooth. Pour it over the veggies and Bake for 20 minutes, stirring every 5 minutes. Serve.

Mushrooms, Sautéed

Servings: 4

Cooking Time: 4 Minutes

Ingredients:

- 8 ounces sliced white mushrooms, rinsed and well drained
- ¼ teaspoon garlic powder
- 1 tablespoon Worcestershire sauce

Directions:

1. Place mushrooms in a large bowl and sprinkle with garlic powder and Worcestershire. Stir well to distribute seasonings evenly.
2. Place in air fryer basket and cook at 390°F for 4 minutes, until tender.

Easy Parmesan Asparagus

Servings: 4

Cooking Time: 15 Minutes

Ingredients:

- 3 tsp grated Parmesan cheese
- 1 lb asparagus, trimmed
- 2 tsp olive oil
- Salt to taste
- 1 clove garlic, minced
- ½ lemon

Directions:

1. Preheat air fryer at 375ºF. Toss the asparagus and olive oil in a bowl, place them in the frying basket, and Air Fry for 8-10 minutes, tossing once. Transfer them into a large serving dish. Sprinkle with salt, garlic, and Parmesan cheese and toss until coated. Serve immediately with a squeeze of lemon. Enjoy!

Rosemary Roasted Potatoes With Lemon

Cooking Time: 12 Minutes

Servings: 4

Ingredients:

- 1 pound small red-skinned potatoes, halved or cut into bite-sized chunks
- 1 tablespoon olive oil
- 1 teaspoon finely chopped fresh rosemary
- ¼ teaspoon salt
- freshly ground black pepper
- 1 tablespoon lemon zest

Directions:

1. Preheat the air fryer to 400°F.
2. Toss the potatoes with the olive oil, rosemary, salt and freshly ground black pepper.
3. Air-fry for 12 minutes (depending on the size of the chunks), tossing the potatoes a few times throughout the cooking process.
4. As soon as the potatoes are tender to a knifepoint, toss them with the lemon zest and more salt if desired.

Lovely Mac`n´cheese

Servings: 4

Cooking Time: 40 Minutes

Ingredients:

- 2 cups grated American cheese
- 4 cups elbow macaroni
- 3 egg, beaten
- ½ cup sour cream
- 4 tbsp butter
- ½ tsp mustard powder
- ½ tsp salt
- 1 cup milk

Directions:

1. Preheat air fryer to 350°F. Bring a pot of salted water to a boil and cook the macaroni following the packet in

structions. Drain and place in a bowl.
2. Add 1 ½ cups of cheese and butter to the hot macaroni and stir to melt. Mix the beaten eggs, milk, sour cream, mustard powder, and salt in a bowl and add the mixture to the macaroni; mix gently. Spoon the macaroni mixture into a greased baking dish and transfer the dish to the air fryer. Bake for 15 minutes. Slide the dish out and sprinkle with the remaining American cheese. Cook for 5-8 more minutes until the top is bubbling and golden. Serve.

Citrusy Brussels Sprouts

Servings: 4

Cooking Time: 15 Minutes

Ingredients:

- 1 lb Brussels sprouts, quartered
- 1 clementine, cut into rings
- 2 garlic cloves, minced
- 1 tbsp olive oil
- 1 tbsp butter, melted
- ½ tsp salt

Directions:

1. Preheat air fryer to 360°F. Add the quartered Brussels sprouts with the garlic, olive oil, butter and salt in a bowl and toss until well coated. Pour the Brussels sprouts into the air fryer, top with the clementine slices, and Roast for 10 minutes. Remove from the air fryer and set the clementines aside. Toss the Brussels sprouts and serve.

Roasted Fennel Salad

Servings: 3

Cooking Time: 20 Minutes

Ingredients:

- 3 cups (about ¾ pound) Trimmed fennel (see the headnote), roughly chopped
- 1½ tablespoons Olive oil
- ¼ teaspoon Table salt
- ¼ teaspoon Ground black pepper
- 1½ tablespoons White balsamic vinegar (see here)

Directions:

1. Preheat the air fryer to 400°F.
2. Toss the fennel, olive oil, salt, and pepper in a large bowl until the fennel is well coated in the oil.
3. When the machine is at temperature, pour the fennel into the basket, spreading it out into as close to one layer as possible. Air-fry for 20 minutes, tossing and rearranging the fennel pieces twice so that any covered or touching parts get exposed to the air currents, until golden at the edges and softened.
4. Pour the fennel into a serving bowl. Add the vinegar while hot. Toss well, then cool a couple of minutes before serving. Or serve at room temperature.

Healthy Caprese Salad

Servings: 2

Cooking Time: 20 Minutes

Ingredients:

- 1 ball mozzarella cheese, sliced
- 16 grape tomatoes
- 2 tsp olive oil
- Salt and pepper to taste
- 1 tbsp balsamic vinegar
- 1 tsp mix of seeds
- 1 tbsp chopped basil

Directions:

1. Preheat air fryer at 350ºF. Toss tomatoes with 1 tsp of olive oil and salt in a bowl. Place them in the frying basket and Air Fry for 15 minutes, shaking twice. Divide mozzarella slices between 2 serving plates, top with blistered tomatoes, and drizzle with balsamic vinegar and the remaining olive oil. Sprinkle with basil, black pepper and the mixed seeds and serve.

Buttered Brussels Sprouts

Servings: 4

Cooking Time: 30 Minutes

Ingredients:

- ¼ cup grated Parmesan
- 2 tbsp butter, melted
- 1 lb Brussels sprouts
- Salt and pepper to taste

Directions:

1. Preheat air fryer to 330°F. Trim the bottoms of the sprouts and remove any discolored leaves. Place the sprouts in a medium bowl along with butter, salt and pepper. Toss to coat, then place them in the frying basket. Roast for 20 minutes, shaking the basket twice. When done, the sprouts should be crisp with golden-brown color. Plate the sprouts in a serving dish and toss with Parmesan cheese.

Sandwiches And Burgers Recipes

Thanksgiving Turkey Sandwiches

Servings: 3

Cooking Time: 10 Minutes

Ingredients:

- 1½ cups Herb-seasoned stuffing mix (not cornbread-style; gluten-free, if a concern)
- 1 Large egg white(s)
- 2 tablespoons Water
- 3 5- to 6-ounce turkey breast cutlets
- Vegetable oil spray
- 4½ tablespoons Purchased cranberry sauce, preferably whole berry
- ⅛ teaspoon Ground cinnamon
- ⅛ teaspoon Ground dried ginger
- 4½ tablespoons Regular, low-fat, or fat-free mayonnaise (gluten-free, if a concern)
- 6 tablespoons Shredded Brussels sprouts
- 3 Kaiser rolls (gluten-free, if a concern), split open

Directions:

1. Preheat the air fryer to 375°F.
2. Put the stuffing mix in a heavy zip-closed bag, seal it, lay it flat on your counter, and roll a rolling pin over the bag to crush the stuffing mix to the consistency of rough sand. (Or you can pulse the stuffing mix to the desired consistency in a food processor.)
3. Set up and fill two shallow soup plates or small pie plates on your counter: one for the egg white(s), whisked with the water until foamy; and one for the ground stuffing mix.
4. Dip a cutlet in the egg white mixture, coating both sides and letting any excess egg white slip back into the rest. Set the cutlet in the ground stuffing mix and coat it evenly on both sides, pressing gently to coat well on both sides. Lightly coat the cutlet on both sides with vegetable oil spray, set it aside, and continue dipping and coating the remaining cutlets in the same way.
5. Set the cutlets in the basket and air-fry undisturbed for 10 minutes, or until crisp and brown. Use kitchen tongs to transfer the cutlets to a wire rack to cool for a few minutes.
6. Meanwhile, stir the cranberry sauce with the cinnamon and ginger in a small bowl. Mix the shredded Brussels sprouts and mayonnaise in a second bowl until the vegetable is evenly coated.
7. Build the sandwiches by spreading about 1½ tablespoons of the cranberry mixture on the cut side of the bottom half of each roll. Set a cutlet on top, then spread about 3 tablespoons of the Brussels sprouts mixture evenly over the cutlet. Set the other half of the roll on top and serve warm.

Perfect Burgers

Servings: 3

Cooking Time: 13 Minutes

Ingredients:

- 1 pound 2 ounces 90% lean ground beef
- 1½ tablespoons Worcestershire sauce (gluten-free, if a concern)
- ½ teaspoon Ground black pepper
- 3 Hamburger buns (gluten-free if a concern), split open

Directions:

1. Preheat the air fryer to 375°F.
2. Gently mix the ground beef, Worcestershire sauce, and pepper in a bowl until well combined but preserving as much of the meat's fibers as possible. Divide this mixture into two 5-inch patties for the small batch, three 5-inch patties for the medium, or four 5-inch patties for the large. Make a thumbprint indentation in the center of each patty, about halfway through the meat.

3. Set the patties in the basket in one layer with some space between them. Air-fry undisturbed for 10 minutes, or until an instant-read meat thermometer inserted into the center of a burger registers 160°F (a medium-well burger). You may need to add 2 minutes cooking time if the air fryer is at 360°F.
4. Use a nonstick-safe spatula, and perhaps a flatware fork for balance, to transfer the burgers to a cutting board. Set the buns cut side down in the basket in one layer (working in batches as necessary) and air-fry undisturbed for 1 minute, to toast a bit and warm up. Serve the burgers in the warm buns.

Salmon Burgers

Servings: 3

Cooking Time: 8 Minutes

Ingredients:

- 1 pound 2 ounces Skinless salmon fillet, preferably fattier Atlantic salmon
- 1½ tablespoons Minced chives or the green part of a scallion
- ½ cup Plain panko bread crumbs (gluten-free, if a concern)
- 1½ teaspoons Dijon mustard (gluten-free, if a concern)
- 1½ teaspoons Drained and rinsed capers, minced
- 1½ teaspoons Lemon juice
- ¼ teaspoon Table salt
- ¼ teaspoon Ground black pepper
- Vegetable oil spray

Directions:

1. Preheat the air fryer to 375°F.
2. Cut the salmon into pieces that will fit in a food processor. Cover and pulse until coarsely chopped. Add the chives and pulse to combine, until the fish is ground but not a paste. Scrape down and remove the blade. Scrape the salmon mixture into a bowl. Add the bread crumbs, mustard, capers, lemon juice, salt, and pepper. Stir gently until well combined.
3. Use clean and dry hands to form the mixture into two 5-inch patties for a small batch, three 5-inch patties for a medium batch, or four 5-inch patties for a large one.
4. Coat both sides of each patty with vegetable oil spray. Set them in the basket in one layer and air-fry undisturbed for 8 minutes, or until browned and an instant-read meat thermometer inserted into the center of a burger registers 145°F.
5. Use a nonstick-safe spatula, and perhaps a flatware fork for balance, to transfer the burgers to a wire rack. Cool for 2 or 3 minutes before serving.

White Bean Veggie Burgers

Servings: 3

Cooking Time: 13 Minutes

Ingredients:

- 1⅓ cups Drained and rinsed canned white beans
- 3 tablespoons Rolled oats (not quick-cooking or steel-cut; gluten-free, if a concern)
- 3 tablespoons Chopped walnuts
- 2 teaspoons Olive oil
- 2 teaspoons Lemon juice
- 1½ teaspoons Dijon mustard (gluten-free, if a concern)

- ¾ teaspoon Dried sage leaves
- ¼ teaspoon Table salt
- Olive oil spray
- 3 Whole-wheat buns or gluten-free whole-grain buns (if a concern), split open

Directions:

1. Preheat the air fryer to 400°F.
2. Place the beans, oats, walnuts, oil, lemon juice, mustard, sage, and salt in a food processor. Cover and process to make a coarse paste that will hold its shape, about like wet sugar-cookie dough, stopping the machine to scrape down the inside of the canister at least once.
3. Scrape down and remove the blade. With clean and wet hands, form the bean paste into two 4-inch patties for the small batch, three 4-inch patties for the medium, or four 4-inch patties for the large batch. Generously coat the patties on both sides with olive oil spray.
4. Set them in the basket with some space between them and air-fry undisturbed for 12 minutes, or until lightly brown and crisp at the edges. The tops of the burgers will feel firm to the touch.
5. Use a nonstick-safe spatula, and perhaps a flatware fork for balance, to transfer the burgers to a cutting board. Set the buns cut side down in the basket in one layer (working in batches as necessary) and air-fry undisturbed for 1 minute, to toast a bit and warm up. Serve the burgers warm in the buns.

Inside Out Cheeseburgers

Servings: 2

Cooking Time: 20 Minutes

Ingredients:

- ¾ pound lean ground beef
- 3 tablespoons minced onion
- 4 teaspoons ketchup
- 2 teaspoons yellow mustard
- salt and freshly ground black pepper
- 4 slices of Cheddar cheese, broken into smaller pieces
- 8 hamburger dill pickle chips

Directions:

1. Combine the ground beef, minced onion, ketchup, mustard, salt and pepper in a large bowl. Mix well to thoroughly combine the ingredients. Divide the meat into four equal portions.
2. To make the stuffed burgers, flatten each portion of meat into a thin patty. Place 4 pickle chips and half of the cheese onto the center of two of the patties, leaving a rim around the edge of the patty exposed. Place the remaining two patties on top of the first and press the meat together firmly, sealing the edges tightly. With the burgers on a flat surface, press the sides of the burger with the palm of your hand to create a straight edge. This will help keep the stuffing inside the burger while it cooks.
3. Preheat the air fryer to 370°F.
4. Place the burgers inside the air fryer basket and air-fry for 20 minutes, flipping the burgers over halfway through the cooking time.
5. Serve the cheeseburgers on buns with lettuce and tomato.

Lamb Burgers

Servings: 3

Cooking Time: 17 Minutes

Ingredients:

- 1 pound 2 ounces Ground lamb
- 3 tablespoons Crumbled feta
- 1 teaspoon Minced garlic
- 1 teaspoon Tomato paste
- ¾ teaspoon Ground coriander
- ¾ teaspoon Ground dried ginger
- Up to ⅛ teaspoon Cayenne
- Up to a ⅛ teaspoon Table salt (optional)
- 3 Kaiser rolls or hamburger buns (gluten-free, if a concern), split open

Directions:

1. Preheat the air fryer to 375°F.
2. Gently mix the ground lamb, feta, garlic, tomato paste, coriander, ginger, cayenne, and salt (if using) in a bowl until well combined, trying to keep the bits of cheese intact. Form this mixture into two 5-inch patties for the small batch, three 5-inch patties for the medium, or four 5-inch patties for the large.
3. Set the patties in the basket in one layer and air-fry undisturbed for 16 minutes, or until an instant-read meat thermometer inserted into one burger registers 160°F. (The cheese is not an issue with the temperature probe in this recipe as it was for the Inside-Out Cheeseburgers, because the feta is so well mixed into the ground meat.)
4. Use a nonstick-safe spatula, and perhaps a flatware fork for balance, to transfer the burgers to a cutting board. Set the buns cut side down in the basket in one layer (working in batches as necessary) and air-fry undisturbed for 1 minute, to toast a bit and warm up. Serve the burgers warm in the buns.

Sausage And Pepper Heros

Servings: 3

Cooking Time: 11 Minutes

Ingredients:

- 3 links (about 9 ounces total) Sweet Italian sausages (gluten-free, if a concern)
- 1½ Medium red or green bell pepper(s), stemmed, cored, and cut into ½-inch-wide strips
- 1 medium Yellow or white onion(s), peeled, halved, and sliced into thin half-moons
- 3 Long soft rolls, such as hero, hoagie, or Italian sub rolls (gluten-free, if a concern), split open lengthwise
- For garnishing Balsamic vinegar
- For garnishing Fresh basil leaves

Directions:

1. Preheat the air fryer to 400°F.
2. When the machine is at temperature, set the sausage links in the basket in one layer and air-fry undisturbed for 5 minutes.
3. Add the pepper strips and onions. Continue air-frying, tossing and rearranging everything about once every minute, for 5 minutes, or until the sausages are browned and an instant-read meat thermometer inserted into one of the links registers 160°F.
4. Use a nonstick-safe spatula and kitchen tongs to transfer the sausages and vegetables to a cutting board. Set the rolls cut side down in the basket in one layer (working in batches as necessary) and air-fry undisturbed for 1 minute, to toast the rolls a bit and warm them up. Set 1 sausage with some pepper strips and onions in each warm roll, sprinkle balsamic vinegar over the sandwich fillings, and garnish with basil leaves.

Chicken Spiedies

Servings: 3

Cooking Time: 12 Minutes

Ingredients:

- 1¼ pounds Boneless skinless chicken thighs, trimmed of any fat blobs and cut into 2-inch pieces
- 3 tablespoons Red wine vinegar
- 2 tablespoons Olive oil
- 2 tablespoons Minced fresh mint leaves
- 2 tablespoons Minced fresh parsley leaves
- 2 teaspoons Minced fresh dill fronds
- ¾ teaspoon Fennel seeds
- ¾ teaspoon Table salt
- Up to a ¼ teaspoon Red pepper flakes
- 3 Long soft rolls, such as hero, hoagie, or Italian sub rolls (gluten-free, if a concern), split open lengthwise
- 4½ tablespoons Regular or low-fat mayonnaise (not fat-free; gluten-free, if a concern)
- 1½ tablespoons Distilled white vinegar
- 1½ teaspoons Ground black pepper

Directions:

1. Mix the chicken, vinegar, oil, mint, parsley, dill, fennel seeds, salt, and red pepper flakes in a zip-closed plastic bag. Seal, gently massage the marinade ingredients into the meat, and refrigerate for at least 2 hours or up to 6 hours. (Longer than that and the meat can turn rubbery.)
2. Set the plastic bag out on the counter (to make the contents a little less frigid). Preheat the air fryer to 400°F.
3. When the machine is at temperature, use kitchen tongs to set the chicken thighs in the basket (discard any remaining marinade) and air-fry undisturbed for 6 minutes. Turn the thighs over and continue air-frying undisturbed for 6 minutes more, until well browned, cooked through, and even a little crunchy.
4. Dump the contents of the basket onto a wire rack and cool for 2 or 3 minutes. Divide the chicken evenly between the rolls. Whisk the mayonnaise, vinegar, and black pepper in a small bowl until smooth. Drizzle this sauce over the chicken pieces in the rolls.

Black Bean Veggie Burgers

Servings: 3

Cooking Time: 10 Minutes

Ingredients:

- 1 cup Drained and rinsed canned black beans
- ⅓ cup Pecan pieces
- ⅓ cup Rolled oats (not quick-cooking or steel-cut; gluten-free, if a concern)
- 2 tablespoons (or 1 small egg) Pasteurized egg substitute, such as Egg Beaters (gluten-free, if a concern)
- 2 teaspoons Red ketchup-like chili sauce, such as Heinz
- ¼ teaspoon Ground cumin
- ¼ teaspoon Dried oregano
- ¼ teaspoon Table salt
- ¼ teaspoon Ground black pepper

- Olive oil
- Olive oil spray

Directions:

1. Preheat the air fryer to 400°F.
2. Put the beans, pecans, oats, egg substitute or egg, chili sauce, cumin, oregano, salt, and pepper in a food processor. Cover and process to a coarse paste that will hold its shape like sugar-cookie dough, adding olive oil in 1-teaspoon increments to get the mixture to blend smoothly. The amount of olive oil is actually dependent on the internal moisture content of the beans and the oats. Figure on about 1 tablespoon (three 1-teaspoon additions) for the smaller batch, with proportional increases for the other batches. A little too much olive oil can't hurt, but a dry paste will fall apart as it cooks and a far-too-wet paste will stick to the basket.
3. Scrape down and remove the blade. Using clean, wet hands, form the paste into two 4-inch patties for the small batch, three 4-inch patties for the medium, or four 4-inch patties for the large batch, setting them one by one on a cutting board. Generously coat both sides of the patties with olive oil spray.
4. Set them in the basket in one layer. Air-fry undisturbed for 10 minutes, or until lightly browned and crisp at the edges.
5. Use a nonstick-safe spatula, and perhaps a flatware fork for balance, to transfer the burgers to a wire rack. Cool for 5 minutes before serving.

Chicken Gyros

Servings: 4

Cooking Time: 14 Minutes

Ingredients:

- 4 4- to 5-ounce boneless skinless chicken thighs, trimmed of any fat blobs
- 2 tablespoons Lemon juice
- 2 tablespoons Red wine vinegar
- 2 tablespoons Olive oil
- 2 teaspoons Dried oregano
- 2 teaspoons Minced garlic
- 1 teaspoon Table salt
- 1 teaspoon Ground black pepper
- 4 Pita pockets (gluten-free, if a concern)
- ½ cup Chopped tomatoes
- ½ cup Bottled regular, low-fat, or fat-free ranch dressing (gluten-free, if a concern)

Directions:

1. Mix the thighs, lemon juice, vinegar, oil, oregano, garlic, salt, and pepper in a zip-closed bag. Seal, gently massage the marinade into the meat through the plastic, and refrigerate for at least 2 hours or up to 6 hours. (Longer than that and the meat can turn rubbery.)
2. Set the plastic bag out on the counter (to make the contents a little less frigid). Preheat the air fryer to 375°F.
3. When the machine is at temperature, use kitchen tongs to place the thighs in the basket in one layer. Discard the marinade. Air-fry the chicken thighs undisturbed for 12 minutes, or until browned and an instant-read meat thermometer inserted into the thickest part of one thigh registers 165°F. You may need to air-fry the chicken 2 minutes longer if the machine's temperature is 360°F.
4. Use kitchen tongs to transfer the thighs to a cutting board. Cool for 5 minutes, then set one thigh in each of the pita pockets. Top each with 2 tablespoons chopped tomatoes and 2 tablespoons dressing. Serve warm.

Reuben Sandwiches

Servings: 2

Cooking Time: 11 Minutes

Ingredients:

- ½ pound Sliced deli corned beef
- 4 teaspoons Regular or low-fat mayonnaise (not fat-free)
- 4 Rye bread slices
- 2 tablespoons plus 2 teaspoons Russian dressing
- ½ cup Purchased sauerkraut, squeezed by the handful over the sink to get rid of excess moisture
- 2 ounces (2 to 4 slices) Swiss cheese slices (optional)

Directions:

1. Set the corned beef in the basket, slip the basket into the machine, and heat the air fryer to 400°F. Air-fry undisturbed for 3 minutes from the time the basket is put in the machine, just to warm up the meat.
2. Use kitchen tongs to transfer the corned beef to a cutting board. Spread 1 teaspoon mayonnaise on one side of each slice of rye bread, rubbing the mayonnaise into the bread with a small flatware knife.
3. Place the bread slices mayonnaise side down on a cutting board. Spread the Russian dressing over the "dry" side of each slice. For one sandwich, top one slice of bread with the corned beef, sauerkraut, and cheese (if using). For two sandwiches, top two slices of bread each with half of the corned beef, sauerkraut, and cheese (if using). Close the sandwiches with the remaining bread, setting it mayonnaise side up on top.
4. Set the sandwich(es) in the basket and air-fry undisturbed for 8 minutes, or until browned and crunchy.
5. Use a nonstick-safe spatula, and perhaps a flatware fork for balance, to transfer the sandwich(es) to a cutting board. Cool for 2 or 3 minutes before slicing in half and serving.

Inside-out Cheeseburgers

Servings: 3

Cooking Time: 9-11 Minutes

Ingredients:

- 1 pound 2 ounces 90% lean ground beef
- ¾ teaspoon Dried oregano
- ¾ teaspoon Table salt
- ¾ teaspoon Ground black pepper
- ¼ teaspoon Garlic powder
- 6 tablespoons (about 1½ ounces) Shredded Cheddar, Swiss, or other semi-firm cheese, or a purchased blend of shredded cheeses
- 3 Hamburger buns (gluten-free, if a concern), split open

Directions:

1. Preheat the air fryer to 375°F.
2. Gently mix the ground beef, oregano, salt, pepper, and garlic powder in a bowl until well combined without turning the mixture to mush. Form it into two 6-inch patties for the small batch, three for the medium, or four for the large.
3. Place 2 tablespoons of the shredded cheese in the center of each patty. With clean hands, fold the sides of the patty up to cover the cheese, then pick it up and roll it gently into a ball to seal the cheese inside. Gently press it back into a 5-inch burger without letting any cheese squish out. Continue filling and preparing more burgers, as needed.

4. Place the burgers in the basket in one layer and air-fry undisturbed for 8 minutes for medium or 10 minutes for well-done. (An instant-read meat thermometer won't work for these burgers because it will hit the mostly melted cheese inside and offer a hotter temperature than the surrounding meat.)
5. Use a nonstick-safe spatula, and perhaps a flatware fork for balance, to transfer the burgers to a cutting board. Set the buns cut side down in the basket in one layer (working in batches as necessary) and air-fry undisturbed for 1 minute, to toast a bit and warm up. Cool the burgers a few minutes more, then serve them warm in the buns.

Chicken Saltimbocca Sandwiches

Servings: 3

Cooking Time: 11 Minutes

Ingredients:

- 3 5- to 6-ounce boneless skinless chicken breasts
- 6 Thin prosciutto slices
- 6 Provolone cheese slices
- 3 Long soft rolls, such as hero, hoagie, or Italian sub rolls (gluten-free, if a concern), split open lengthwise
- 3 tablespoons Pesto, purchased or homemade (see the headnote)

Directions:

1. Preheat the air fryer to 400°F.
2. Wrap each chicken breast with 2 prosciutto slices, spiraling the prosciutto around the breast and overlapping the slices a bit to cover the breast. The prosciutto will stick to the chicken more readily than bacon does.
3. When the machine is at temperature, set the wrapped chicken breasts in the basket and air-fry undisturbed for 10 minutes, or until the prosciutto is frizzled and the chicken is cooked through.
4. Overlap 2 cheese slices on each breast. Air-fry undisturbed for 1 minute, or until melted. Take the basket out of the machine.
5. Smear the insides of the rolls with the pesto, then use kitchen tongs to put a wrapped and cheesy chicken breast in each roll.

Best-ever Roast Beef Sandwiches

Servings: 6

Cooking Time: 30-50 Minutes

Ingredients:

- 2½ teaspoons Olive oil
- 1½ teaspoons Dried oregano
- 1½ teaspoons Dried thyme
- 1½ teaspoons Onion powder
- 1½ teaspoons Table salt
- 1½ teaspoons Ground black pepper
- 3 pounds Beef eye of round
- 6 Round soft rolls, such as Kaiser rolls or hamburger buns (gluten-free, if a concern), split open lengthwise
- ¾ cup Regular, low-fat, or fat-free mayonnaise (gluten-free, if a concern)
- 6 Romaine lettuce leaves, rinsed

- 6 Round tomato slices (¼ inch thick)

Directions:

1. Preheat the air fryer to 350°F.
2. Mix the oil, oregano, thyme, onion powder, salt, and pepper in a small bowl. Spread this mixture all over the eye of round.
3. When the machine is at temperature, set the beef in the basket and air-fry for 30 to 50 minutes (the range depends on the size of the cut), turning the meat twice, until an instant-read meat thermometer inserted into the thickest piece of the meat registers 130°F for rare, 140°F for medium, or 150°F for well-done.
4. Use kitchen tongs to transfer the beef to a cutting board. Cool for 10 minutes. If serving now, carve into ⅛-inch-thick slices. Spread each roll with 2 tablespoons mayonnaise and divide the beef slices between the rolls. Top with a lettuce leaf and a tomato slice and serve. Or set the beef in a container, cover, and refrigerate for up to 3 days to make cold roast beef sandwiches anytime.

Eggplant Parmesan Subs

Servings: 2

Cooking Time: 13 Minutes

Ingredients:

- 4 Peeled eggplant slices (about ½ inch thick and 3 inches in diameter)
- Olive oil spray
- 2 tablespoons plus 2 teaspoons Jarred pizza sauce, any variety except creamy
- ¼ cup (about ⅔ ounce) Finely grated Parmesan cheese
- 2 Small, long soft rolls, such as hero, hoagie, or Italian sub rolls (gluten-free, if a concern), split open lengthwise

Directions:

1. Preheat the air fryer to 350°F.
2. When the machine is at temperature, coat both sides of the eggplant slices with olive oil spray. Set them in the basket in one layer and air-fry undisturbed for 10 minutes, until lightly browned and softened.
3. Increase the machine's temperature to 375°F (or 370°F, if that's the closest setting—unless the machine is already at 360°F, in which case leave it alone). Top each eggplant slice with 2 teaspoons pizza sauce, then 1 tablespoon cheese. Air-fry undisturbed for 2 minutes, or until the cheese has melted.
4. Use a nonstick-safe spatula, and perhaps a flatware fork for balance, to transfer the eggplant slices cheese side up to a cutting board. Set the roll(s) cut side down in the basket in one layer (working in batches as necessary) and air-fry undisturbed for 1 minute, to toast the rolls a bit and warm them up. Set 2 eggplant slices in each warm roll.

Chicken Apple Brie Melt

Servings: 3

Cooking Time: 13 Minutes

Ingredients:

- 3 5- to 6-ounce boneless skinless chicken breasts
- Vegetable oil spray
- 1½ teaspoons Dried herbes de Provence
- 3 ounces Brie, rind removed, thinly sliced
- 6 Thin cored apple slices

- 3 French rolls (gluten-free, if a concern)
- 2 tablespoons Dijon mustard (gluten-free, if a concern)

Directions:

1. Preheat the air fryer to 375°F.
2. Lightly coat all sides of the chicken breasts with vegetable oil spray. Sprinkle the breasts evenly with the herbes de Provence.
3. When the machine is at temperature, set the breasts in the basket and air-fry undisturbed for 10 minutes.
4. Top the chicken breasts with the apple slices, then the cheese. Air-fry undisturbed for 2 minutes, or until the cheese is melty and bubbling.
5. Use a nonstick-safe spatula and kitchen tongs, for balance, to transfer the breasts to a cutting board. Set the rolls in the basket and air-fry for 1 minute to warm through. (Putting them in the machine without splitting them keeps the insides very soft while the outside gets a little crunchy.)
6. Transfer the rolls to the cutting board. Split them open lengthwise, then spread 1 teaspoon mustard on each cut side. Set a prepared chicken breast on the bottom of a roll and close with its top, repeating as necessary to make additional sandwiches. Serve warm.

Thai-style Pork Sliders

Servings: 4

Cooking Time: 15 Minutes

Ingredients:

- 11 ounces Ground pork
- 2½ tablespoons Very thinly sliced scallions, white and green parts
- 4 teaspoons Minced peeled fresh ginger
- 2½ teaspoons Fish sauce (gluten-free, if a concern)
- 2 teaspoons Thai curry paste (see the headnote; gluten-free, if a concern)
- 2 teaspoons Light brown sugar
- ¾ teaspoon Ground black pepper
- 4 Slider buns (gluten-free, if a concern)

Directions:

1. Preheat the air fryer to 375°F.
2. Gently mix the pork, scallions, ginger, fish sauce, curry paste, brown sugar, and black pepper in a bowl until well combined. With clean, wet hands, form about ⅓ cup of the pork mixture into a slider about 2½ inches in diameter. Repeat until you use up all the meat—3 sliders for the small batch, 4 for the medium, and 6 for the large. (Keep wetting your hands to help the patties adhere.)
3. When the machine is at temperature, set the sliders in the basket in one layer. Air-fry undisturbed for 14 minutes, or until the sliders are golden brown and caramelized at their edges and an instant-read meat thermometer inserted into the center of a slider registers 160°F.
4. Use a nonstick-safe spatula, and perhaps a flatware fork for balance, to transfer the sliders to a cutting board. Set the buns cut side down in the basket in one layer (working in batches as necessary) and air-fry undisturbed for 1 minute, to toast a bit and warm up. Serve the sliders warm in the buns.

Mexican Cheeseburgers

Servings: 4

Cooking Time: 22 Minutes

Ingredients:

- 1¼ pounds ground beef
- ¼ cup finely chopped onion
- ½ cup crushed yellow corn tortilla chips
- 1 (1.25-ounce) packet taco seasoning
- ¼ cup canned diced green chilies
- 1 egg, lightly beaten
- 4 ounces pepper jack cheese, grated
- 4 (12-inch) flour tortillas
- shredded lettuce, sour cream, guacamole, salsa (for topping)

Directions:

1. Combine the ground beef, minced onion, crushed tortilla chips, taco seasoning, green chilies, and egg in a large bowl. Mix thoroughly until combined – your hands are good tools for this. Divide the meat into four equal portions and shape each portion into an oval-shaped burger.
2. Preheat the air fryer to 370°F.
3. Air-fry the burgers for 18 minutes, turning them over halfway through the cooking time. Divide the cheese between the burgers, lower fryer to 340°F and air-fry for an additional 4 minutes to melt the cheese. (This will give you a burger that is medium-well. If you prefer your cheeseburger medium-rare, shorten the cooking time to about 15 minutes and then add the cheese and proceed with the recipe.)
4. While the burgers are cooking, warm the tortillas wrapped in aluminum foil in a 350°F oven, or in a skillet with a little oil over medium-high heat for a couple of minutes. Keep the tortillas warm until the burgers are ready.
5. To assemble the burgers, spread sour cream over three quarters of the tortillas and top each with some shredded lettuce and salsa. Place the Mexican cheeseburgers on the lettuce and top with guacamole. Fold the tortillas around the burger, starting with the bottom and then folding the sides in over the top. (A little sour cream can help hold the seam of the tortilla together.) Serve immediately.

Dijon Thyme Burgers

Servings: 3

Cooking Time: 18 Minutes

Ingredients:

- 1 pound lean ground beef
- ⅓ cup panko breadcrumbs
- ¼ cup finely chopped onion
- 3 tablespoons Dijon mustard
- 1 tablespoon chopped fresh thyme
- 4 teaspoons Worcestershire sauce
- 1 teaspoon salt
- freshly ground black pepper
- Topping (optional):
- 2 tablespoons Dijon mustard
- 1 tablespoon dark brown sugar
- 1 teaspoon Worcestershire sauce
- 4 ounces sliced Swiss cheese, optional

Directions:

1. Combine all the burger ingredients together in a large bowl and mix well. Divide the meat into 4 equal portions and then form the burgers, being careful not to over-handle the meat. One good way to do this is to throw the meat back and forth from one hand to another, packing the meat each time you catch it. Flatten the

balls into patties, making an indentation in the center of each patty with your thumb (this will help it stay flat as it cooks) and flattening the sides of the burgers so that they will fit nicely into the air fryer basket.
2. Preheat the air fryer to 370°F.
3. If you don't have room for all four burgers, air-fry two or three burgers at a time for 8 minutes. Flip the burgers over and air-fry for another 6 minutes.
4. While the burgers are cooking combine the Dijon mustard, dark brown sugar, and Worcestershire sauce in a small bowl and mix well. This optional topping to the burgers really adds a boost of flavor at the end. Spread the Dijon topping evenly on each burger. If you cooked the burgers in batches, return the first batch to the cooker at this time – it's ok to place the fourth burger on top of the others in the center of the basket. Air-fry the burgers for another 3 minutes.
5. Finally, if desired, top each burger with a slice of Swiss cheese. Lower the air fryer temperature to 330°F and air-fry for another minute to melt the cheese. Serve the burgers on toasted brioche buns, dressed the way you like them.

Chicken Club Sandwiches

Servings: 3

Cooking Time: 15 Minutes

Ingredients:

- 3 5- to 6-ounce boneless skinless chicken breasts
- 6 Thick-cut bacon strips (gluten-free, if a concern)
- 3 Long soft rolls, such as hero, hoagie, or Italian sub rolls (gluten-free, if a concern)
- 3 tablespoons Regular, low-fat, or fat-free mayonnaise (gluten-free, if a concern)
- 3 Lettuce leaves, preferably romaine or iceberg
- 6 ¼-inch-thick tomato slices

Directions:

1. Preheat the air fryer to 375°F.
2. Wrap each chicken breast with 2 strips of bacon, spiraling the bacon around the meat, slightly overlapping the strips on each revolution. Start the second strip of bacon farther down the breast but on a line with the start of the first strip so they both end at a lined-up point on the chicken breast.
3. When the machine is at temperature, set the wrapped breasts bacon-seam side down in the basket with space between them. Air-fry undisturbed for 12 minutes, until the bacon is browned, crisp, and cooked through and an instant-read meat thermometer inserted into the center of a breast registers 165°F. You may need to add 2 minutes in the air fryer if the temperature is at 360°F.
4. Use kitchen tongs to transfer the breasts to a wire rack. Split the rolls open lengthwise and set them cut side down in the basket. Air-fry for 1 minute, or until warmed through.
5. Use kitchen tongs to transfer the rolls to a cutting board. Spread 1 tablespoon mayonnaise on the cut side of one half of each roll. Top with a chicken breast, lettuce leaf, and tomato slice. Serve warm.

Desserts And Sweets

Vanilla Butter Cake

Servings: 6

Cooking Time: 20-24 Minutes

Ingredients:

- ¾ cup plus 1 tablespoon All-purpose flour
- 1 teaspoon Baking powder
- ¼ teaspoon Table salt
- 8 tablespoons (½ cup/1 stick) Butter, at room temperature
- ½ cup Granulated white sugar
- 2 Large egg(s)
- 2 tablespoons Whole or low-fat milk (not fat-free)
- ¾ teaspoon Vanilla extract
- Baking spray (see here)

Directions:

1. Preheat the air fryer to 325°F (or 330°F, if that's the closest setting).
2. Mix the flour, baking powder, and salt in a small bowl until well combined.
3. Using an electric hand mixer at medium speed, beat the butter and sugar in a medium bowl until creamy and smooth, about 3 minutes, occasionally scraping down the inside of the bowl.
4. Beat in the egg or eggs, as well as the white or a yolk as necessary. Beat in the milk and vanilla until smooth. Turn off the beaters and add the flour mixture. Beat at low speed until thick and smooth.
5. Use the baking spray to generously coat the inside of a 6-inch round cake pan for a small batch, a 7-inch round cake pan for a medium batch, or an 8-inch round cake pan for a large batch. Scrape and spread the batter into the pan, smoothing the batter out to an even layer.
6. Set the pan in the basket and air-fry undisturbed for 20 minutes for a 6-inch layer, 22 minutes for a 7-inch layer, or 24 minutes for an 8-inch layer, or until a toothpick or cake tester inserted into the center of the cake comes out clean. Start checking it at the 15-minute mark to know where you are.
7. Use hot pads or silicone baking mitts to transfer the cake pan to a wire rack. Cool for 5 minutes. To unmold, set a cutting board over the baking pan and invert both the board and the pan. Lift the still-warm pan off the cake layer. Set the wire rack on top of the cake layer and invert all of it with the cutting board so that the cake layer is now right side up on the wire rack. Remove the cutting board and continue cooling the cake for at least 10 minutes or to room temperature, about 30 minutes, before slicing into wedges.

Peanut Butter S'mores

Servings: 10

Cooking Time: 1 Minute

Ingredients:

- 10 Graham crackers (full, double-square cookies as they come out of the package)
- 5 tablespoons Natural-style creamy or crunchy peanut butter
- ½ cup Milk chocolate chips
- 10 Standard-size marshmallows (not minis and not jumbo campfire ones)

Directions:

1. Preheat the air fryer to 350°F.
2. Break the graham crackers in half widthwise at the marked place, so the rectangle is now in two squares. Set half of the squares flat side up on your work surface. Spread each with about 1½ teaspoons peanut butter, then set 10 to 12 chocolate chips point side up into the peanut butter on each, pressing gently so the chips stick.
3. Flatten a marshmallow between your clean, dry hands and set it atop the chips. Do the same with the remaining marshmallows on the other coated graham crackers. Do not set the other half of the graham crackers on top of these coated graham crackers.
4. When the machine is at temperature, set the treats graham cracker side down in a single layer in the basket. They may touch, but even a fraction of an inch between them will provide better air flow. Air-fry undisturbed for 45 seconds.
5. Use a nonstick-safe spatula to transfer the topped graham crackers to a wire rack. Set the other graham cracker squares flat side down over the marshmallows. Cool for a couple of minutes before serving.

Peanut Butter-banana Roll-ups

Servings: 4

Cooking Time: 20 Minutes

Ingredients:

- 2 ripe bananas, halved crosswise
- 4 spring roll wrappers
- ¼ cup molasses
- ¼ cup peanut butter
- 1 tsp ground cinnamon
- 1 tsp lemon zest

Directions:

1. Preheat air fryer to 375°F. Place the roll wrappers on a flat surface with one corner facing up. Spread 1 tbsp of molasses on each, then 1 tbsp of peanut butter, and finally top with lemon zest and 1 banana half. Sprinkle with cinnamon all over. For the wontons, fold the bottom over the banana, then fold the sides, and roll-up. Place them seam-side down and Roast for 10 minutes until golden brown and crispy. Serve warm.

Coconut-carrot Cupcakes

Servings: 4

Cooking Time: 25 Minutes

Ingredients:

- 1 cup flour
- ½ tsp baking soda
- 1/3 cup light brown sugar
- ¼ tsp salt
- ¼ tsp ground cinnamon
- 1 ½ tsp vanilla extract
- 1 egg
- 1 tbsp buttermilk
- 1 tbsp vegetable oil

- ¼ cup grated carrots
- 2 tbsp coconut shreds
- 6 oz cream cheese
- 1 1/3 cups powdered sugar
- 2 tbsp butter, softened
- 1 tbsp milk
- 1 tbsp coconut flakes

Directions:

1. Preheat air fryer at 375ºF. Combine flour, baking soda, brown sugar, salt, and cinnamon in a bowl. In another bowl, combine egg, 1 tsp of vanilla, buttermilk, and vegetable oil. Pour wet ingredients into dry ingredients and toss to combine. Do not overmix. Fold in carrots and coconut shreds. Spoon mixture into 8 greased silicone cupcake liners. Place cupcakes in the frying basket and Bake for 6-8 minutes. Let cool onto a cooling rack for 15 minutes. Whisk cream cheese, powdered sugar, remaining vanilla, softened butter, and milk in a bowl until smooth. Spread over cooled cupcakes. Garnish with coconut flakes and serve.

Cinnamon Canned Biscuit Donuts

Servings: 4

Cooking Time: 25 Minutes

Ingredients:

- 1 can jumbo biscuits
- 1 cup cinnamon sugar

Directions:

1. Preheat air fryer to 360°F. Divide biscuit dough into 8 biscuits and place on a flat work surface. Cut a small circle in the center of the biscuit with a small cookie cutter. Place a batch of 4 donuts in the air fryer. Spray with oil and Bake for 8 minutes, flipping once. Drizzle the cinnamon sugar over the donuts and serve.

Fall Pumpkin Cake

Servings: 6

Cooking Time: 50 Minutes

Ingredients:

- 1/3 cup pecan pieces
- 5 gingersnap cookies
- 1/3 cup light brown sugar
- 6 tbsp butter, melted
- 3 eggs
- ½ tsp vanilla extract
- 1 cup pumpkin purée
- 2 tbsp sour cream
- ½ cup flour
- ¼ cup tapioca flour
- ½ tsp cornstarch
- ½ cup granulated sugar
- ½ tsp baking soda
- 1 tsp baking powder

- 1 tsp pumpkin pie spice
- 6 oz mascarpone cheese
- 1 1/3 cups powdered sugar
- 1 tsp cinnamon
- 2 tbsp butter, softened
- 1 tbsp milk
- 1 tbsp flaked almonds

Directions:

1. Blitz the pecans, gingersnap cookies, brown sugar, and 3 tbsp of melted butter in a food processor until combined. Press mixture into the bottom of a lightly greased cake pan. Preheat air fryer at 350°F. In a bowl, whisk the eggs, remaining melted butter, ½ tsp of vanilla extract, pumpkin purée, and sour cream. In another bowl combine the flour, tapioca flour, cornstarch, granulated sugar, baking soda, baking powder, and pumpkin pie spice. Add wet ingredients to dry ingredients and combine. Do not overmix. Pour the batter into a cake pan and cover it with aluminum foil. Place cake pan in the frying basket and Bake for 30 minutes. Remove the foil and cook for another 5 minutes. Let cool onto a cooling rack for 10 minutes. Then, turn cake onto a large serving platter. In a small bowl, whisk the mascarpone cheese, powdered sugar, remaining vanilla extract, cinnamon, softened butter, and milk. Spread over cooled cake and cut into slices. Serve sprinkled with almonds and enjoy!

Orange Gooey Butter Cake

Servings: 6

Cooking Time: 85 Minutes

Ingredients:

- Crust Layer:
- ½ cup flour
- ¼ cup sugar
- ½ teaspoon baking powder
- ⅛ teaspoon salt
- 2 ounces (½ stick) unsalted European style butter, melted
- 1 egg
- 1 teaspoon orange extract
- 2 tablespoons orange zest
- Gooey Butter Layer:
- 8 ounces cream cheese, softened
- 4 ounces (1 stick) unsalted European style butter, melted
- 2 eggs
- 2 teaspoons orange extract
- 2 tablespoons orange zest
- 4 cups powdered sugar
- Garnish:
- powdered sugar
- orange slices

Directions:

1. Preheat the air fryer to 350°F.
2. Grease a 7-inch cake pan and line the bottom with parchment paper. Combine the flour, sugar, baking powder, and salt in a bowl. Add the melted butter, egg, orange extract and orange zest. Mix well and press this mixture into the bottom of the greased cake pan. Lower the pan into the basket using an aluminum foil sling (fol

a piece of aluminum foil into a strip about 2-inches wide by 24-inches long). Fold the ends of the aluminum foil over the top of the dish before returning the basket to the air fryer. Air-fry uncovered for 8 minutes.
3. To make the gooey butter layer, beat the cream cheese, melted butter, eggs, orange extract and orange zest in a large bowl using an electric hand mixer. Add the powdered sugar in stages, beat until smooth with each addition. Pour this mixture on top of the baked crust in the cake pan. Wrap the pan with a piece of greased aluminum foil, tenting the top of the foil to leave a little room for the cake to rise.
4. Air-fry for 60 minutes at 350°F. Remove the aluminum foil and air-fry for an additional 17 minutes.
5. Let the cake cool inside the pan for at least 10 minutes. Then, run a butter knife around the cake and let the cake cool completely in the pan. When cooled, run the butter knife around the edges of the cake again and invert it onto a plate and then back onto a serving platter. Sprinkle the powdered sugar over the top of the cake and garnish with orange slices.

Giant Oatmeal-peanut Butter Cookie

Servings: 4

Cooking Time: 18 Minutes

Ingredients:

- 1 cup Rolled oats (not quick-cooking or steel-cut oats)
- ½ cup All-purpose flour
- ½ teaspoon Ground cinnamon
- ½ teaspoon Baking soda
- ⅓ cup Packed light brown sugar
- ¼ cup Solid vegetable shortening
- 2 tablespoons Natural-style creamy peanut butter
- 3 tablespoons Granulated white sugar
- 2 tablespoons (or 1 small egg, well beaten) Pasteurized egg substitute, such as Egg Beaters
- ⅓ cup Roasted, salted peanuts, chopped
- Baking spray

Directions:

1. Preheat the air fryer to 350°F.
2. Stir the oats, flour, cinnamon, and baking soda in a bowl until well combined.
3. Using an electric hand mixer at medium speed, beat the brown sugar, shortening, peanut butter, granulated white sugar, and egg substitute or egg (as applicable) until smooth and creamy, about 3 minutes, scraping down the inside of the bowl occasionally.
4. Scrape down and remove the beaters. Fold in the flour mixture and peanuts with a rubber spatula just until all the flour is moistened and the peanut bits are evenly distributed in the dough.
5. For a small air fryer, coat the inside of a 6-inch round cake pan with baking spray. For a medium air fryer, coat the inside of a 7-inch round cake pan with baking spray. And for a large air fryer, coat the inside of an 8-inch round cake pan with baking spray. Scrape and gently press the dough into the prepared pan, spreading it into an even layer to the perimeter.
6. Set the pan in the basket and air-fry undisturbed for 18 minutes, or until well browned.
7. Transfer the pan to a wire rack and cool for 15 minutes. Loosen the cookie from the perimeter with a spatula, then invert the pan onto a cutting board and let the cookie come free. Remove the pan and reinvert the cookie onto the wire rack. Cool for 5 minutes more before slicing into wedges to serve.

Cheese & Honey Stuffed Figs

Servings: 4

Cooking Time: 15 Minutes

Ingredients:

- 8 figs, stem off
- 2 oz cottage cheese
- ¼ tsp ground cinnamon
- ¼ tsp orange zest
- ¼ tsp vanilla extract
- 2 tbsp honey
- 1 tbsp olive oil

Directions:

1. Preheat air fryer to 360°F. Cut an "X" in the top of each fig 1/3 way through, leaving intact the base. Mix together the cottage cheese, cinnamon, orange zest, vanilla extract and 1 tbsp of honey in a bowl. Spoon the cheese mixture into the cavity of each fig. Put the figs in a single layer in the frying basket. Drizzle the olive oil over the top of the figs and Roast for 10 minutes. Drizzle with the remaining honey. Serve and enjoy!

Party S'mores

Servings: 6

Cooking Time: 15 Minutes

Ingredients:

- 2 dark chocolate bars, cut into 12 pieces
- 12 buttermilk biscuits
- 12 marshmallows

Directions:

1. Preheat air fryer to 350°F. Place 6 biscuits in the air fryer. Top each square with a piece of dark chocolate. Bake for 2 minutes. Add a marshmallow to each piece of chocolate. Cook for another minute. Remove and top with another piece of biscuit. Serve warm.

Baked Apple

Servings: 6

Cooking Time: 20 Minutes

Ingredients:

- 3 small Honey Crisp or other baking apples
- 3 tablespoons maple syrup
- 3 tablespoons chopped pecans
- 1 tablespoon firm butter, cut into 6 pieces

Directions:

1. Put ½ cup water in the drawer of the air fryer.
2. Wash apples well and dry them.
3. Split apples in half. Remove core and a little of the flesh to make a cavity for the pecans.
4. Place apple halves in air fryer basket, cut side up.
5. Spoon 1½ teaspoons pecans into each cavity.
6. Spoon ½ tablespoon maple syrup over pecans in each apple.

7. Top each apple with ½ teaspoon butter.
8. Cook at 360°F for 20 minutes, until apples are tender.

Easy Bread Pudding

Servings: 4

Cooking Time: 25 Minutes

Ingredients:

- 2 cups sandwich bread cubes
- ½ cup pecan pieces
- ½ cup raisins
- 3 eggs
- ¼ cup half-and-half
- ¼ cup dark corn syrup
- 1 tsp vanilla extract
- 2 tbsp bourbon
- 2 tbsp dark brown sugar
- ¼ tsp ground cinnamon
- ½ tsp nutmeg
- ¼ tsp salt

Directions:

1. Preheat air fryer at 325ºF. Spread the bread pieces in a cake pan and layer pecan pieces and raisins over the top. Whisk the eggs, half-and-half, corn syrup, bourbon, vanilla extract, sugar, cinnamon, nutmeg, and salt in a bowl. Pour egg mixture over pecan pieces. Let sit for 10 minutes. Place the cake pan in the frying basket and Bake for 15 minutes. Let cool onto a cooling rack for 10 minutes before slicing. Serve immediately.

Coconut-custard Pie

Servings: 4

Cooking Time: 20 Minutes

Ingredients:

- 1 cup milk
- ¼ cup plus 2 tablespoons sugar
- ¼ cup biscuit baking mix
- 1 teaspoon vanilla
- 2 eggs
- 2 tablespoons melted butter
- cooking spray
- ½ cup shredded, sweetened coconut

Directions:

1. Place all ingredients except coconut in a medium bowl.
2. Using a hand mixer, beat on high speed for 3 minutes.
3. Let sit for 5 minutes.
4. Preheat air fryer to 330°F.
5. Spray a 6-inch round or 6 x 6-inch square baking pan with cooking spray and place pan in air fryer basket.
6. Pour filling into pan and sprinkle coconut over top.

7. Cook pie at 330°F for 20 minutes or until center sets.

Air-fried Strawberry Hand Tarts

Servings: 9

Cooking Time: 9 Minutes

Ingredients:

- ½ cup butter, softened
- ½ cup sugar
- 2 eggs
- 1 teaspoon vanilla extract
- 2 tablespoons lemon zest
- 2½ cups all-purpose flour
- 1 teaspoon baking powder
- ¼ teaspoon salt
- 1¼ cups strawberry jam, divided
- 1 egg white, beaten
- 1 cup powdered sugar
- 2 teaspoons milk

Directions:

1. Combine the butter and sugar in a bowl and beat with an electric mixer until the mixture is light and fluffy. Add the eggs one at a time. Add the vanilla extract and lemon zest and mix well. In a separate bowl, combine the flour, baking powder and salt. Add the dry ingredients to the wet ingredients, mixing just until the dough comes together. Transfer the dough to a floured surface and knead by hand for 10 minutes. Cover with a clean kitchen towel and let the dough rest for 30 minutes. (Alternatively, dough can be mixed and kneaded in a stand mixer.)
2. Divide the dough in half and roll each half out into a ¼-inch thick rectangle that measures 12-inches x 9-inches. Cut each rectangle of dough into nine 4-inch x 3-inch rectangles (a pizza cutter is very helpful for this task). You should have 18 rectangles. Spread two teaspoons of strawberry jam in the center of nine of the rectangles leaving a ¼-inch border around the edges. Brush the egg white around the edges of each rectangle and top with the remaining nine rectangles of dough. Press the back of a fork around the edges to seal the tarts shut. Brush the top of the tarts with the beaten egg white and pierce the dough three or four times down the center of the tart with a fork.
3. Preheat the air fryer to 350°F.
4. Air-fry the tarts in batches at 350°F for 6 minutes. Flip the tarts over and air-fry for an additional 3 minutes.
5. While the tarts are air-frying, make the icing. Combine the powdered sugar, ¼ cup strawberry preserves and milk in a bowl, whisking until the icing is smooth. Spread the icing over the top of each tart, leaving an empty border around the edges. Decorate with sprinkles if desired.

Caramel Apple Crumble

Servings: 6

Cooking Time: 50 Minutes

Ingredients:

- 4 apples, peeled and thinly sliced
- 2 tablespoons sugar

- 1 tablespoon flour
- 1 teaspoon ground cinnamon
- ¼ teaspoon ground allspice
- healthy pinch ground nutmeg
- 10 caramel squares, cut into small pieces
- Crumble Topping:
- ¾ cup rolled oats
- ¼ cup sugar
- ⅓ cup flour
- ¼ teaspoon ground cinnamon
- 6 tablespoons butter, melted

Directions:

1. Preheat the air fryer to 330°F.
2. Combine the apples, sugar, flour, and spices in a large bowl and toss to coat. Add the caramel pieces and mix well. Pour the apple mixture into a 1-quart round baking dish that will fit in your air fryer basket (6-inch diameter).
3. To make the crumble topping, combine the rolled oats, sugar, flour and cinnamon in a small bowl. Add the melted butter and mix well. Top the apples with the crumble mixture. Cover the entire dish with aluminum foil and transfer the dish to the air fryer basket, lowering the dish into the basket using a sling made of aluminum foil (fold a piece of aluminum foil into a strip about 2-inches wide by 24-inches long). Fold the ends of the aluminum foil over the top of the dish before returning the basket to the air fryer.
4. Air-fry at 330°F for 25 minutes. Remove the aluminum foil and continue to air-fry for another 25 minutes. Serve the crumble warm with whipped cream or vanilla ice cream, if desired.

Fried Pineapple Chunks

Servings: 3

Cooking Time: 10 Minutes

Ingredients:

- 3 tablespoons Cornstarch
- 1 Large egg white, beaten until foamy
- 1 cup (4 ounces) Ground vanilla wafer cookies (not low-fat cookies)
- ¼ teaspoon Ground dried ginger
- 18 (about 2¼ cups) Fresh 1-inch chunks peeled and cored pineapple

Directions:

1. Preheat the air fryer to 400°F.
2. Put the cornstarch in a medium or large bowl. Put the beaten egg white in a small bowl. Pour the cookie crumbs and ground dried ginger into a large zip-closed plastic bag, shaking it a bit to combine them.
3. Dump the pineapple chunks into the bowl with the cornstarch. Toss and stir until well coated. Use your cleaned fingers or a large fork like a shovel to pick up a few pineapple chunks, shake off any excess cornstarch, and put them in the bowl with the egg white. Stir gently, then pick them up and let any excess egg white slip back into the rest. Put them in the bag with the crumb mixture. Repeat the cornstarch-then-egg process until all the pineapple chunks are in the bag. Seal the bag and shake gently, turning the bag this way and that, to coat the pieces well.
4. Set the coated pineapple chunks in the basket with as much air space between them as possible. Even a fraction of an inch will work, but they should not touch. Air-fry undisturbed for 10 minutes, or until golden brown and crisp.
5. Gently dump the contents of the basket onto a wire rack. Cool for at least 5 minutes or up to 15 minutes be-

fore serving.

Oreo-coated Peanut Butter Cups

Servings: 8

Cooking Time: 4 Minutes

Ingredients:

- 8 Standard ¾-ounce peanut butter cups, frozen
- ⅓ cup All-purpose flour
- 2 Large egg white(s), beaten until foamy
- 16 Oreos or other creme-filled chocolate sandwich cookies, ground to crumbs in a food processor
- Vegetable oil spray

Directions:

1. Set up and fill three shallow soup plates or small pie plates on your counter: one for the flour, one for the beaten egg white(s), and one for the cookie crumbs.
2. Dip a frozen peanut butter cup in the flour, turning it to coat all sides. Shake off any excess, then set it in the beaten egg white(s). Turn it to coat all sides, then let any excess egg white slip back into the rest. Set the candy bar in the cookie crumbs. Turn to coat on all parts, even the sides. Dip the peanut butter cup back in the egg white(s) as before, then into the cookie crumbs as before, making sure you have a solid, even coating all around the cup. Set aside while you dip and coat the remaining cups.
3. When all the peanut butter cups are dipped and coated, lightly coat them on all sides with the vegetable oil spray. Set them on a plate and freeze while the air fryer heats.
4. Preheat the air fryer to 400°F.
5. Set the dipped cups wider side up in the basket with as much air space between them as possible. Air-fry undisturbed for 4 minutes, or until they feel soft but the coating is set.
6. Turn off the machine and remove the basket from it. Set aside the basket with the fried cups for 10 minutes. Use a nonstick-safe spatula to transfer the fried cups to a wire rack. Cool for at least another 5 minutes before serving.

Carrot-oat Cake Muffins

Servings: 4

Cooking Time: 20 Minutes

Ingredients:

- 3 tbsp butter, softened
- ¼ cup brown sugar
- 1 tbsp maple syrup
- 1 egg white
- ½ tsp vanilla extract
- 1/3 cup finely grated carrots
- ½ cup oatmeal
- 1/3 cup flour
- ½ tsp baking soda
- ¼ cup raisins

Directions:

1. Preheat air fryer to 350°F. Mix the butter, brown sugar, and maple syrup until smooth, then toss in the eg

white, vanilla, and carrots. Whisk well and add the oatmeal, flour, baking soda, and raisins. Divide the mixture between muffin cups. Bake in the fryer for 8-10 minutes.

Blueberry Cheesecake Tartlets

Servings: 9

Cooking Time: 6 Minutes

Ingredients:

- 8 ounces cream cheese, softened
- ¼ cup sugar
- 1 egg
- ½ teaspoon vanilla extract
- zest of 2 lemons, divided
- 9 mini graham cracker tartlet shells*
- 2 cups blueberries
- ½ teaspoon ground cinnamon
- juice of ½ lemon
- ¼ cup apricot preserves

Directions:

1. Preheat the air fryer to 330°F.
2. Combine the cream cheese, sugar, egg, vanilla and the zest of one lemon in a medium bowl and blend until smooth by hand or with an electric hand mixer. Pour the cream cheese mixture into the tartlet shells.
3. Air-fry 3 tartlets at a time at 330°F for 6 minutes, rotating them in the air fryer basket halfway through the cooking time.
4. Combine the blueberries, cinnamon, zest of one lemon and juice of half a lemon in a bowl. Melt the apricot preserves in the microwave or over low heat in a saucepan. Pour the apricot preserves over the blueberries and gently toss to coat.
5. Allow the cheesecakes to cool completely and then top each one with some of the blueberry mixture. Garnish the tartlets with a little sugared lemon peel and refrigerate until you are ready to serve.

Donut Holes

Servings: 13

Cooking Time: 12 Minutes

Ingredients:

- 6 tablespoons Granulated white sugar
- 1½ tablespoons Butter, melted and cooled
- 2 tablespoons (or 1 small egg, well beaten) Pasteurized egg substitute, such as Egg Beaters
- 6 tablespoons Regular or low-fat sour cream (not fat-free)
- ¾ teaspoon Vanilla extract
- 1⅔ cups All-purpose flour
- ¾ teaspoon Baking powder
- ¼ teaspoon Table salt
- Vegetable oil spray

Directions:

1. Preheat the air fryer to 350°F.
2. Whisk the sugar and melted butter in a medium bowl until well combined. Whisk in the egg substitute or egg, then the sour cream and vanilla until smooth. Remove the whisk and stir in the flour, baking powder, and salt with a wooden spoon just until a soft dough forms.
3. Use 2 tablespoons of this dough to create a ball between your clean palms. Set it aside and continue making balls: 8 more for the small batch, 12 more for the medium batch, or 17 more for the large one.
4. Coat the balls in the vegetable oil spray, then set them in the basket with as much air space between them as possible. Even a fraction of an inch will be enough, but they should not touch. Air-fry undisturbed for 12 minutes, or until browned and cooked through. A toothpick inserted into the center of a ball should come out clean.
5. Pour the contents of the basket onto a wire rack. Cool for at least 5 minutes before serving.

INDEX

A

Air-fried Strawberry Hand Tarts	102
Apple French Toast Sandwich	13
Arancini With Marinara	70
Asparagus	76

B

Bacon, Broccoli And Swiss Cheese Bread Pudding	17
Baked Apple	100
Baked Eggs With Bacon-tomato Sauce	15
Balsamic Green Beans With Bacon	77
Balsamic Marinated Rib Eye Steak With Balsamic Fried Cipollini Onions	45
Banana-strawberry Cakecups	16
Basic Chicken Breasts(1)	41
Beef Al Carbon (street Taco Meat)	44
Best-ever Roast Beef Sandwiches	90
Black Bean Veggie Burgers	87
Blueberry Cheesecake Tartlets	105
Blueberry French Toast Sticks	19
Bread Boat Eggs	20
Breaded Parmesan Perch	54
Breakfast Burrito With Sausage	19
Breakfast Chimichangas	20
Buttered Brussels Sprouts	82
Buttered Chicken Thighs	34
Buttered Turkey Breasts	39
Buttery Radish Wedges	77

C

Cajun Chicken Livers	40
Caponata Salsa	21
Caramel Apple Crumble	102
Carrot-oat Cake Muffins	104
Cheddar & Egg Scramble	17
Cheese & Honey Stuffed Figs	99
Cheese Ravioli	65
Cheese Straws	29
Cheese Wafers	29
Cheesy Eggplant Lasagna	72
Cheesy Salmon-stuffed Avocados	53
Cheesy Veggie Frittata	67
Chicken Apple Brie Melt	91
Chicken Club Sandwiches	94
Chicken Gyros	88
Chicken Meatballs With A Surprise	37
Chicken Saltimbocca Sandwiches	90
Chicken Spiedies	87
Chinese-style Lamb Chops	44
Chinese-style Potstickers	28
Cinnamon Canned Biscuit Donuts	97
Cinnamon Pear Oat Muffins	16
Citrusy Brussels Sprouts	81

Coconut-carrot Cupcakes	96
Coconut-custard Pie	101
Corn & Shrimp Boil	52
Corn And Pepper Jack Chile Rellenos With Roasted Tomato Sauce	71
Country Chicken Hoagies	36
Crab Cake Bites	24
Crispy "fried" Chicken	33
Crispy Ham And Eggs	51
Crunchy Rice Paper Samosas	66

D

Dijon Thyme Burgers	93
Dilly Red Snapper	56
Donut Holes	106

E

Easy Asian-style Tuna	59
Easy Bread Pudding	101
Easy Caprese Flatbread	14
Easy Carnitas	48
Easy Parmesan Asparagus	79
Egg Rolls	72
Eggless Mung Bean Tart	18
Eggplant Parmesan Subs	91

F

Falafels	63
Fall Pumpkin Cake	97
Farmer's Fried Chicken	33
Fiery Chicken Meatballs	31
Fish And "chips"	61
Fish Tacos With Hot Coleslaw	58
Five Spice Fries	22
Fried Eggplant Balls	77
Fried Pineapple Chunks	103
Fried Scallops	55

G

Garlic Bread Knots	13
Garlic Breadsticks	30
Garlicky Bell Pepper Mix	74
General Tso's Cauliflower	68
Giant Oatmeal–peanut Butter Cookie	99
Glazed Chicken Thighs	37
Green Dip With Pine Nuts	79
Green Onion Pancakes	18
Grilled Ham & Muenster Cheese On Raisin Bread	27

H

Harissa Chicken Wings	40
Harissa Veggie Fries	69
Healthy Caprese Salad	82
Holiday Shrimp Scampi	61
Honey-lemon Chicken Wings	22
Horseradish Tuna Croquettes	60
Hot Calamari Rings	59

I

Indonesian Pork Satay	44
Inside Out Cheeseburgers	85
Inside-out Cheeseburgers	89
Intense Buffalo Chicken Wings	32

K

Kale Chips	28
Kielbasa Chunks With Pineapple & Peppers	49
Kochukaru Pork Lettuce Cups	49

L

Lamb Burger With Feta And Olives	50
Lamb Burgers	85
Lemon-blueberry Morning Bread	11
Lemon-dill Salmon Burgers	62
Lime Halibut Parcels	57
Lovely Mac`n´cheese	80

M

Maple Bacon Wrapped Chicken Breasts	36
Meat Loaves	42
Mexican Cheeseburgers	92
Middle Eastern Phyllo Rolls	26
Middle Eastern Roasted Chickpeas	27
Mom´s Tuna Melt Toastie	55
Mushrooms, Sautéed	79

N

Nutty Whole Wheat Muffins	15

O

Orange Gooey Butter Cake	98
Oreo-coated Peanut Butter Cups	104

P

Party Giant Nachos	62
Party S´mores	100
Patatas Bravas	78
Peachy Pork Chops	51
Peanut Butter S'mores	95
Peanut Butter-banana Roll-ups	96
Perfect Burgers	83
Philly Chicken Cheesesteak Stromboli	32
Piña Colada Shrimp	57
Pineapple & Veggie Souvlaki	69
Pizza Dough	12
Poblano Bake	38
Polenta Fries With Chili-lime Mayo	30
Poppy Seed Mini Hot Dog Rolls	24
Punjabi-inspired Chicken	39

R

Red Curry Flank Steak	47
Reuben Sandwiches	89
Rich Baked Sweet Potatoes	78
Rigatoni With Roasted Onions, Fennel, Spinach And Lemon Pepper Ricotta	73
Roasted Fennel Salad	81
Roasted Veggie Bowls	67
Rosemary Roasted Potatoes With Lemon	80

S

Salmon Burgers	84
Salmon Puttanesca En Papillotte With Zucchini	53
Sausage & Cauliflower Balls	25
Sausage And Pepper Heros	86
Seared Scallops In Beurre Blanc	59
Sesame Carrots And Sugar Snap Peas	76

Shrimp-jalapeño Poppers In Prosciutto	54
Sinaloa Fish Fajitas	56
Sirloin Steak Flatbread	43
Skirt Steak Fajitas	42
Skirt Steak With Horseradish Cream	48
Spiced Pumpkin Wedges	75
Spicy Black Bean Turkey Burgers With Cumin-avocado Spread	37
Spicy Chicken And Pepper Jack Cheese Bites	21
Spinach & Brie Frittata	65
Steak Fajitas	52
Steakhouse Burgers With Red Onion Compote	46
Stress-free Beef Patties	46
Sunday Chicken Skewers	35
Sushi-style Deviled Eggs	64
Sweet Chili Peanuts	27
Sweet Potato–crusted Pork Rib Chops	41

T

Tamari-seasoned Pork Strips	47
Teriyaki Chicken Bites	35
Teriyaki Tofu With Spicy Mayo	75
Thai-style Pork Sliders	92
Thanksgiving Turkey Sandwiches	82
Thyme Beef & Eggs	11
Thyme Sweet Potato Wedges	74
Tilapia Al Pesto	60
Tropical Salsa	70

V

Vanilla Butter Cake	95
Vegetable Spring Rolls	23
Vegetarian Fritters With Green Dip	23
Vegetarian Shepherd's Pie	64
Veggie Samosas	67
Vietnamese Gingered Tofu	63

W

Wake-up Veggie & Ham Bake	12
Warm And Salty Edamame	25
Western Frittata	14
White Bean Veggie Burgers	84

Y

Yummy Maple-mustard Chicken Kabobs	34

Printed in Great Britain
by Amazon

57369104R00062